CW00348078

SERVING GOD
AND
GOD'S CREATURES

A memorial volume to celebrate the life of
Frederick Pratt Green

Born 2 September 1903

Died 22 October 2000

Bernard Braley

*Dedicated to all who travelled alongside Fred
during his 97 mortal years*

*Commissioned by The Pratt Green Trust
and published for them
by*

Stainer & Bell
London
2001

British Library Cataloguing-in-Publication Data
A catalogue record of this book is available from the British Library

ISBN 0 85249 865 9

Cover design by Keith Wakefield. The collage is taken from photographs in the book
supplemented with Smoke, one of the Greens' much beloved cats.

Other books by Bernard Braley published by Stainer & Bell Ltd:

Hymnwriters 1
(Thomas Ken; William Cowper; Reginald Heber; William Walsham How; John Ellerton)

Hymnwriters 2
(Henry Baker; Albert Bayly; James Montgomery; John Newton)

Hymnwriters 3
(George Herbert; Edward Hayes Plumptre; Robert Bridges; Fred Pratt Green)

Worship and Where We Work

Anthologies by Fred Pratt Green in print:

The Hymns and Ballads of Fred Pratt Green, Later Hymns and Ballads and Fifty Poems, The Last Lap
The above are jointly published by Stainer & Bell and (for USA and Canada) Hope Publishing Company USA.

A biography of Fred Pratt Green will be found in Braley: **Hymnwriters 3** (Stainer & Bell) – see above

Out of print anthologies by Fred Pratt Green:

26 Hymns, This Unlikely Earth, The Skating Parson, The Old Couple

All except a few hymn texts of local interest will be found on the CD-ROM **HymnQuest**
at present available in Great Britain and Ireland from Stainer & Bell.

Fred Pratt Green's 51 hymn-writing scrapbooks are lodged at Emory University, Atlanta, USA
with copies in the United Kingdom in The Pratt Green Hymnology Collection at the University of Durham.

A complete bibliography of Fred Pratt Green's individual hymns, poems, plays
and other writing is being prepared and should be available on the 2002 edition of *HymnQuest.*
Enquiries may be addressed by post only to Fred Pratt Green's Literary Executor,
Bernard Braley, 191 Creighton Avenue, London, N2 9BN England.

In due course, it is hoped to deposit either the originals or copies of the majority of Fred Pratt Green's
papers now held by the Literary Executor with the University of Durham, or Emory University.

Printed in Great Britain by Caligraving Ltd, Thetford

CONTENTS

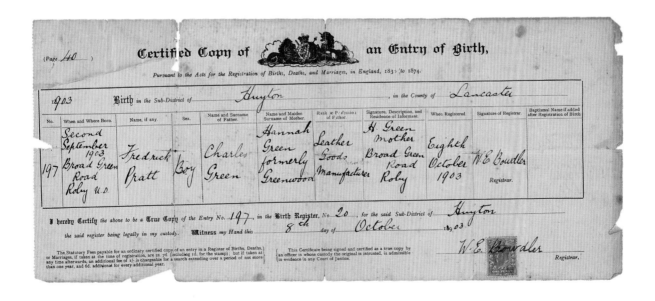

THE LIFE AND WORK OF

FREDERICK PRATT GREEN

Fred after receiving his M.B.E. from the Lord Lieutenant of Norfolk

Photograph by Jacqueline Wyatt

FOREWORD BY ALAN LUFF

Canon Alan Luff

Joan and Bernard Braley outside their London
residence, of which Fred wrote in his diary: 'I fit
into their routine easily and enjoy the relaxed
atmosphere of their home. They never fuss.'

It was in 1969 that I, like most of us who sing hymns, came across the name of Fred Pratt Green. For me it was at a meeting of the Hymn Society in Liverpool, at which we were introduced to two slim hymn-book supplements, *100 Hymns for Today* from *Hymns Ancient and Modern*, and *Hymns and Songs*, the Methodist publication. It was the new texts in those volumes which excited me; I had been working in the sixties with the Dunblane Music Consultation, set up by the Scottish Churches Council, and it was always new words that we looked for, often in vain.

So who were the bright young men and women who were producing the new texts in these supplements? To my astonishment, in the Anglican book certainly the most interesting texts were from people whose dates of birth hovered around 1900. Where had they been before? In some cases the answer was that the writers' work had not been valued. In the case of the one who was to contribute over the next fifteen years a flood of fine hymns the answer was that he had not been writing hymns until then. Those who cared about such things knew his name as a poet. Methodists knew him as one of their ministers for his distinguished and imaginative ministry.

For the wider world, both in Britain, and increasingly in America, somehow Fred Pratt Green sprang into our consciousness at the age of 66. The fruit of those years up till then was shown in his writing from then on, but what those years contained we did not know.

The Trustees have therefore asked Bernard Braley, a founder Trustee, to answer the question 'Who was Fred Pratt Green?', and to give us some clues as to how he was prepared, one must say, by the long foresight of the grace of God, for those years of hymn-writing ministry that have so benefited and blessed the English-speaking churches and those others who have received his hymns in translation.

Alan Luff   Cardiff
Chair of The Pratt Green Trust   4 January 2001

1

PROLOGUE

Tell us all how the most gifted Methodist hymn-writer since Charles Wesley suddenly emerged from hiding in the last laps of his life. That is the essence of the brief laid down for this book by the Trustees of The Pratt Green Trust.

In large measure, this can be done best in Fred's own words and through remembrances of just a few of the many whose lives touched his own over the 97 years of his life. It is the extraordinary story of an ordinary man, and of his relationship with God and God's creatures. It is a story of countless partnerships. Fred wore L-plates all his life, learning from all whom he met and to whom he gave counsel or encouragement, or with whom he just had a good laugh. It was a life of growing experience of the nature, the mystery, the truth of God, whom he met in friends and neighbours, in artists, scientists and philosophers, from earliest to contemporary writers, and from the natural world.

Primarily it was a partnership with a creative God who dwells among us, revealing in the Cross that God was a suffering servant–companion of each human journey, alive today and laughing and crying with the human creatures of every generation. Humble in the search for Truth, aware of the numinous in every aspect of living, Fred was constantly grateful that his knowledge of God found a Supreme Being whom he could know as Love. He rejoiced with the apostle Peter on the seashore that when he, too, denied his Lord, he was given another chance to serve.

> One morning on that misty shore
> We found a meal prepared,
> And ate together one meal more
> With him, our risen Lord.
>
> Three times he asked me, face to face,
> If I were still his man.
> It's thanks to his amazing grace,
> Yes, I am still his man!
>
> And if you, too, deny your Lord,
> Although it be but once,
> You'll hear the same forgiving word
> And have your second chance.
>
> For some are called a second time
> And some more times than this;
> And only those who follow him
> Know what all others miss.

Written by Fred Pratt Green for the tune AMAZING GRACE

What I do know is that the creative spirit in Man (apologies to women!), responsible for nuclear weapons as well as for artistic achievement and social improvement, is *God in us*. And shall God die? My deepest conviction is expressed in a poem I wrote many years ago *Question and Answer*...It declares that the meaning of life is to be found in what I call *Creativity*. God is himself creating a new Heaven and a new Earth, and in this task we are able to share, in ways that are plainly and even spectacularly beneficial to the human race, but also in the simplest but necessary tasks of everyday life. *We are all artists* – each in our own sphere. To have been creative in poetry, yes and even in hymn writing, is the greatest of all privileges. To God be the glory!

From Notebook, 5 August 1985

BIRTH

At an Edwardian home in Broad Green Road in the Lancashire village of Roby, to Charles Green, Liverpool leather goods manufacturer, and Shropshire lass Hannah Green, née Greenwood, the gift of a third child, Frederick Pratt Green, a laughing, crying possibility, a brother for Marjorie and Osborne.

To Frederick Pratt Green, the gift of a Christian home, not over-pious parents – they only went to church once on Sunday, rather than twice like the thoroughly devout – *a mixed blessing* (like all parents).

To Frederick Pratt Green, the gift of genes from ancestors of countless generations, a unique creature fashioned with all human beings, in the words of ancient Hebrew priests, *in the image of God.*

Of Fred's ancestors, he noted only two others in the manuscripts known to me: his paternal and maternal grandmothers. Fred wrote, when considering what made him tick: *I can hear the two clocks chiming together in my carcase, detect the McCartney in me, playing at cat with the Billington mouse.*

It is appropriate here and there in this volume to add words by Fred's contemporaries. In his diaries, he acknowledged the part played by Sydney Carter in breaking the mould of what might be sung in Church. As publisher to both, I found a greater rapport with them than with all the others it was a privilege to know and publish. I found in some ways a remarkable similarity between the two men. Sacred to both were truth, integrity and creativity seen in myriad forms in everyday men and women. Sydney was exploring God in quantum physics in his early eighties. Fred was not; yet he was equally aware of the presence of God in science and mathematics.

I am your laughing, crying,
possibility:
I keep on coming as
I did before,

hoping and hungering
and with no visible
means of support
whatever.

Naked need is
all I offer:
my extremity is
your opportunity,

my Bethlehem
is where you can be born,
And will you be
King Herod to yourself?

Look in the mirror of
my cradle, see
your laughing, crying,
possibility,

hoping and hungering
and with no visible
means of support
whatever.

Sydney Carter: *Child*

I asked the plum-tree: is there a purpose?
Weighed down by a crop heavy as grief,
It answered, 'The purpose is to be a tree.
What other purpose could there be?'
But I watched it sicken of silver-leaf.

I asked the willow-warbler: is there a purpose?
Young innocent in the thorny brake,
It answered, 'The purpose is to be a bird.
What other purpose could there be?'
But I saw no mercy in the eye of the snake.

I asked my blood-brother: is there a purpose?
Busy at his craft in the sun-washed room,
He answered, 'The purpose is to be a man.
What other purpose could there be?'
When they called him to breakfast he did not come.

I asked the Hidden One: is there a purpose?
Dear and doomed in brother and bird and tree,
He answered, 'The purpose is creativity.
What other purpose could there be?
Am I not creating you – and you Me?'

Fred Pratt Green: *Question and Answer*. Written in 1952

The Harvest Festival is not, of course, a Christian festival. It has its roots in the elemental experience which preceded the organised faiths. A pagan festival? But not to me! The whole conception of God the creator and sustainer of the universe and everything in it, and of the evolutionary process, even of a Wordsworthian pantheism, is very important to me. The meaning of life is CREATIVITY: this is my fundamental belief.

What God created 'in the beginning' is the great and mysterious preliminary to 'the salvation of the world through Christ'. Yes. A noble faith, not to be narrowed into an exclusive orthodoxy.

So I enjoyed our Harvest Festival service this morning at Chapel Field. The church was 'decorated' to illustrate 'We plough the fields...' very broadly interpreted. Close to me was a mural on HEALTH, with a nice pamphlet above my head on HOW TO REDUCE YOUR WEIGHT!!

Fred Pratt Green: *Diary 1987*

The most interesting thing today didn't happen to me but to Marjorie... Her [group] usually deals with some topic of the day or with some aspect of church life. Last meeting, Marjorie introduced the subject of parental authority and hardly got a word in. Tonight a member gave a long, quite technical account of 'genetic engineering' (or 'messing about with the foetus'), which left little time and not much encouragement for discussion.

Imagine such a subject had it been possible, being discussed even twenty-five years ago! As far as I understand the issues, like the Pope, I am against it!

Fred Pratt Green: diary entry headed *Foetus*. Written in 1987

GRANDMOTHERS AND MOTHER

My grandmothers McCartney and Billington
Ticked in our lives like the two clocks
We were proudest of in our Liverpool home.

The dining-room clock was of black marble,
Bold-faced and pilastered, with a loud
Tick and an imperiously metallic strike;

But the drawing-room clock was a confection
Of whispering wheels in a glass case,
Prettily gilded, with a silvery-soft voice.

What a contrast they made, my grandmothers
McCartney and Billington, one too buxom
In black silk, one petite in white lace!

My father's mother had been married thrice;
Bossy in a house full of bric-a-brac,
She died, out shopping, at twelve o'clock.

My mother's mother had been married twice;
The beloved relict of a drunken lay-about,
She lived with us, mousily, for ten years,

And stealthily departed after sipping milk
Laced with brandy. At times, when I stop
To ask myself what it is makes me tick,

I can hear the two clocks chiming together
In my carcase, detect the McCartney in me
Playing at cat with the Billington mouse.

Fred Pratt Green: *Grandmothers*. Published 1976

In his diaries, Fred names a number of people whose influence he considered was especially benign. The first-named on the list was his mother, from whom he inherited a peace-loving disposition and sensitivity. At home, while Father thought he was in charge, Mother was the one who quietly ruled early home life.

Among the books still on Fred's shelves when he died was a copy of *Cookery and Domestic Economy for Young Housewives*, presented to Hannah Greenwood in 1887. Fred enjoyed his food; and he would certainly have regarded the work of his mother's cooking and managing the household budget as exercising her gift of creativity.

Inside the book were the notes Fred made for a talk given in 1948 on *A Book for Victorian Housewives*. I have not found any sermon notes from the days of his itinerant ministry among his papers, but reproduce these notes as an illustration of how he developed a theme.

Hannah Green

HOW THE BOOK CAME INTO MY POSSESSION
I go home. A wet afternoon. I hunt for a book to read. 'The Journals of Queen Victoria', 'The Conquest of the Air', 'Enquire Within', 'Card Sharping' – *the thin green book*, with no title visible.

COOKERY FOR YOUNG HOUSEWIVES
Published 1838. 25th edition 1875. *The inscription:* 'Hannah Greenwood, with best wishes from N. H. 24th October 1887.' *The explanation:* given to my mother when she went into service. 'I had to learn how to carve, dear.'

THE TRAGEDY OF THE VICTORIAN AGE
1887 – what was life like in 1887? What was happening in England?
Politics: Year of Victoria's first jubilee. General Gordon murdered at Khartoum in 1885. Defeat of the Liberals and of Gladstone's Home Rule Bill. Conservatism has triumphed!
Social Conditions: Severe depressions in trade, with occasional booms. *The appalling poverty and misery* of great mass of industrial & agricultural workers.
Charles Booth has revealed state of affairs in London. 32% of population in chronic poverty; 1,250,000 in actual poverty. Grave unrest in London: the new Conservative Government has banned meetings in Trafalgar Square.
November 13th 1887: 'Bloody Sunday'. The police use bludgeons against peaceful demonstration making its way to the Square. Bobbie Burns is imprisoned for his share...
The Victorian Age was a glorious age: but it had a dark aspect. *The social irresponsibility of the privileged classes.* The position of the Domestic Servant. 'Skivvy', 'slavvy': female domestic servant.

THE BOOK PROVIDES ME WITH AMUSEMENT
A most delightful and amusing book. And quite instructive! So refreshing in an age of rationing!
How to make a Rice Pudding p.90: Steak p.27: Cleaning a Brussels Carpet p.133: Instructions about the Gas p.134: A Bill of Fare for 12 persons p.121. Yet the book is for the Middle Class 'less affluent'. The preface: *This book is a Manual of plain directions to be used in the kitchens of the middle or less affluent classes; the endeavour is to shew how tasteful and nutritious dishes may be prepared at little expense in order to render home happy and attractive.*

THE VIRTUE OF THE VICTORIAN AGE
It was the age of *FAMILY LIFE* – of the *HOME*. In spite of its restrictiveness, the Victorian home of the Middle Class had much to commend it.

THE VICTORIAN HOUSEWIFE as pictured in this book. No credit! p.128. Solitude! p.130.

THE THREE PRINCIPLES OF THE VICTORIAN HOUSEWIFE
1. *Do everything in its proper time.* The sense of order. The quiet efficiency. *Time for Religion.*
2. *Keep everything to its proper use.* The principle is an excellent one – and how we break it. The misuse of all we have invented since 1887! We do not put our lives to the proper use!
3. *Put everything in its proper place.* A good principle but liable to abuse. The proper place for servants is in the attic and below stairs. Where shall we put God? God was in *His* place.

LAST WORD
The pendulum has swung far! Many wrongs have been put right – and much freedom has been gained...

BUT SOMETHING HAS BEEN LOST
Has discipline been lost? Has the love of the home been lost? Has the good vanished with the evil?
I steal the book... 1887–1948. Sixty-one years. *What will 2009 think of us?*
'How absurd to think that anyone will want to listen to such a talk...'

Fred Pratt Green: notes for a talk entitled *A Book for Victorian Housewives*

Fred's early playmates lived at a nearby farm. His mother had been brought up in the Church of England. There being no nearby Methodist chapel, on Sunday mornings the family walked over the fields to All Saints Church at Childwall. Very little of the original eleventh-century building remains, although the main part of the church survives from the fifteenth century. Readers who have a chance to visit it should find there notes by David Street, including a plan of the building at the time Fred attended worship.

> My hymns of childhood were in A & M,
> bound tightly to the Book of Common Prayer.
> Summoned by bells, like the young Betjeman,
> we hurry over fields to Childwall, where
> we have to worship God, arriving just
> before the last bell warns us we are late.
> The church is beautiful and crowded. Hushed,
> forbidden even to whisper, we must wait
> for a door to open… Daring to look,
> I crane my neck to see the cross go by,
> as we all sing a long hymn in our book.
> And you, who write processionals, know why
> to worship means what it has always meant:
> this sense of sharing in a Great Event.

Fred Pratt Green: *Sonnet for Canon J. E. Bowers*

When Fred was eight, he was taken to see an uncle who was disabled by the loss of his right hand. The incident is described vividly in the following poem:

When you are eight, and you are old enough
Not to stare at a cripple, not to look back,
Not to ask loud questions then and there,
We shall take you, they said, to see Jack,
Poor Jack, they said, as they looked where
There was nothing to look at, and their lips
Stopped talking, shutting up like mousetraps
Because I was not old enough, I was there.

So when I was eight, and I was old enough
To feed spiders with flies, to feel fear
Prickle the back of my neck, nobody near,
We must take you, they said, to see Jack,
Poor Jack, they said, but be sure not to stare
At his right hand, if he kisses you forget
Who it is, if he speaks to you answer back
Politely, say it is a fine day or a wet.

The day was fine, with thunder in the air,
As we drove from the door with a whip-crack,
Gee-up, whoa-there! Now you are old enough
We are taking you, they said, to see Jack,
Poor Jack, they said, who sits in a chair
All day, all year, watching her, or asleep
Like a child, no use to her, and bringing
Nothing in, doing nothing to earn his keep.

We walked to a cottage, down a rutted lane
Hedged with holly, wicked with nettles, sure
Of finding him in, they said, because Jack,
Poor Jack, has a sickness nobody can cure,
And whatever you do, they said, don't stare
At his right hand, but if he holds it out
Take it, shake it politely, it won't bite,
And accept nothing, only an apple or pear.

Where sunflowers glared at us over a fence
We are here, they said, stroking my hair
To comfort me, seeing Jack was asleep there
In the doorway, with his head lolling back,
And his right hand, small as a baby's, limp,
Dangling, for a hand is nothing to fear
And more use, they had said, than a stump.
But you can't teach the heart not to stare.

Fred Pratt Green: *You can't teach the heart not to stare*

Worship continued at Childwall Church until 1912.

All Saints Church today

Then the family moved to Wallasey and worshipped on Sunday mornings at Claremont Road Wesleyan Methodist Church. Fred attended Wallasey Grammar School, where a school friend, Eric Thomas is described by Fred as the second especially benign influence in his life. Eric became an ordained priest of the Church of England and, when Fred married Marjorie in 1931, he was best man and a signatory in the Marriage Register. He can be seen in the wedding photograph on page 28.

Today, hearing of your death, I remember
how we slugged each other with satchels,
your cut lip sealing our friendship; how,
between games of bagatelle we slaughtered
tin soldiers, as flags moved backwards
on the sagging map towards disaster; how
we built sand-castles, and abandoned them
to the invading tide, like tired Romans
called home to defend nearer frontiers; how
we lazed in warm hollows among the sand-
dunes, screened by scratchy marron-grass,
furtively probing each other's defences
until we reached the perimeters of alarm,
and drew back; how life parted us, without
cutting the thread, so that for thirty years
we wrote at Christmas, yet without meeting,
until, time pressing, I crossed your path
(you were standing outside a shop, smiling,
clerically benign); how, paralysed by sadness
I drove on. I cannot believe that you are dead.

Fred Pratt Green: *Ten Friends: In Memoriam E.W.T.*

17 Beresford Road photographed when
Fred went to review his childhood home

RYDAL

In April 1917 the Americans entered the First World War. By August, the third battle of Ypres raged in the Flanders quagmire, with heavy casualties. Fred, at the age of 14, started boarding at a Methodist school in North Wales, from where he wrote the following letter in his first term:

Rydal Mount School
<u>Colwyn Bay</u>

<u>1/12/17</u>

Dear Mother & Father

I have been having a very 'fast' week. On Wednesday night Rydal Mount choir gave a concert to a large audience in St John's schoolroom. It was very good indeed, I sang in 4 songs.

On Thursday night the Head gave a lecture on the 'War in the Air' with some very interesting lantern slides.

And above all yesterday (Friday) was the Cadet whole. At 9.30 in the morning with our water-bottles & 5 biscuits we began a whole days outting, the whole cadet corps of 93 boys set out for Llanryst, just fancy. We reached there at 1.30 after a very hard march over the mountains, the roads being frightfully muddy and very hard to march on, however we had a good time and we were quite cheerful. Mr Costain marched with us the whole of the way, talking to us and cheering us on – even singing himself, like a true chaplin. The other 2 officers also came. The distance was <u>16 miles</u> practically all up <u>steep</u> hills. When we got there we had a light lunch, where ever we liked to go I had a plate of bread and butter, a drink of coffee, some jam and a nice rest for 7d, simply splendid.

We had from 1.30-6.30 off. I spent my time in the library, going in the neighbouring church which were splendid and going by the side of the Conway river. I had 2/- to live on. At 6.45, the cadets caught the train to Colwyn Bay and when we got home, we found a topping supper for us, consisting of beef, cocoa and good bread and butter not mentioning Mrs Costain's smiling face. We were dead tired and the Head made us all bathe our feet in hot water, after which we got in bed and slept till 7.15 this morning. I feel fresh as a daisy. Tonight we are having a lantern lecture on the 'Scenery of England'.

I was playing for the Schools 4th eleven against Tan-y-bryn school but the match has been put off for the weather is bad, so the first chance I might have had of playing for the school is lost.

Now having no more to say I will leave off. Remember me to Mrs Elkes and Mrs Hill & give my best kisses and love to yourselves and Marjorie and Osborn. Only 17 days more.

Your loving son

Fred

Spelling and punctuation unchanged: 49 kisses, divided between his parents and siblings, completed the last page.

The third especially benign influence named by Fred in his diaries was the schoolmaster A. G. Watt. Fred clearly caught much of Watt's philosophy of living; and I reproduce from *The Rydalian* a substantial part of a tribute paid to him on his eventual retirement over three decades later. Watt also fostered in his pupil a lifelong interest in history and a love of poetry. Fred cites Milton's *Lycidas* as the poem which first inspired his interest in the art. The school magazine included his first two published poems, *Rydal* and later *To an Unknown Warrior*.

A. G. WATT: INFLUENTIAL SCHOOLMASTER

There are some who are expert window-dressers. Their talents are few, but they have an unbounded satisfaction in them, and a flair for self-advertisement, so that sometimes they go far and many near to them wish that they would go farther. To the fraternity of these showmen Mr Watt has never belonged. He has an astonishing humility and, perhaps, he has erred on the other side. It is the nobler error and, after all, they are but poor attainments that need a trumpeter.

A. G. Watt

He has never flaunted a learning that is wide and deep, and free from the aridity that sometimes mars the scholar. Many of his colleagues have felt the stimulus of that learning, and have kindled their little candles from the lamp of his scholarship, for no man has been quicker to share with others the riches of his mind. To those with everything to learn about the art of teaching, and humbly aware of that fact, he has been a tower of strength, and a patient and a kindly counsellor. To him they have owed the avoidance of the pitfalls into which the inexperienced so easily fall, and out of which it is so desperately difficult for them to climb again. It meant much to Rydal that there was a man of Mr Watt's intellectual stature and quick human sympathies when Mr Costain was gathering his staff about him at the beginning of his headmastership. Have we accepted too easily his unfailing courtesy to all of us, and the gentleness that has stood the strain of many different kinds of provocation? He has always preferred the role of the peacemaker to that of the stirrer-up of strife, and his voice is not one of those that are raised in hoarse dispute.

He might so easily have gone the way of the University don, and there were those who urged him to do just that, and who saw in him the occupant of a professorial chair. He had no desire to live that kind of life, for he knew that it would take him away from boys, and it was amongst boys that he felt that his work lay. There are hundreds of Rydalians who would gratefully acknowledge that he was right, for, if he had thought otherwise, they would have been deprived of one of the great stimulating influences of their lives.

It is impossible to think of Mr Watt without thinking of Old House, for above everything else, he has been a Housemaster, and probably he has found the keenest pleasure of his calling in the visits paid to his dormitories each night, and in the pleasant relationships established with his boys. Even the black sheep among them (and there have been a number) have had the grace to know that in him they had a friend. It has been that knowledge that has drawn them to his room in large numbers on their return to the school as Old Rydalians, to sit by his fireside until late into the night and tell him all about themselves in the certain knowledge that he really cared to hear. He is a living denial of the theory that boys respect most those of their masters who are proficient in games, for no man knows less of sport or has less interest in it, and yet no man has a surer hold on their affections. The truth of the matter is that the young are shrewd judges of character, and that in Mr Watt they have recognized one who was prepared to live out his religion in his relationships with them. Perhaps, sometimes, he has worried over-much and driven himself too hard, when a less conscientious man would have taken his ease and saved himself some vexation of spirit. That is not a modern failing, and there is a great gulf set between those who care deeply and those who could not care less.

Extract from *The Rydalian*

POETRY AND HISTORY

In Memory of A.G.W.

You taught the Shell what History it knew,
Using, if you remember, coloured chalks
Out of a tin box to illustrate your talks:
Red, sir, for vital facts and figures; blue
For whatever gains an extra mark; yellow
For all that must be argued. To this day
The Merry Monarch is red, poor Nelly blue.
History, thanks to you, was never grey.

You were eccentric, sir, and awfully bald.
Flapping about in front of a blackboard
You might have been an excitable blackbird
Defnding its territory. So time crawled
Rarely for us, sir. We admired the way,
As you explained it, some obscure affray
Of the Roses had blossomed in red and yellow.
History, thanks to you, was never grey.

We dug for pottery while the other stayed
Cheering on chilly touch-lines. Off the cuff,
You lacked *esprit de corps*; you used to scoff
At flannelled players lounging in the shade
On summer afternoons; but you could chuck
A piece of coloured chalk better than they
A cricket ball, and knock the bails off us.
History, thanks to you, was never grey.

History, since your time, has lost its grip,
Grows more horrific or completely crazy.
You would have greeted with Gilbertian glee
Orbital flights and trips in a space-ship
To stellar worlds. Sir, didn't you once cry:
I need black chalk for St. Bartholomew's Day?
What would you need for Belsen and the Bomb?
History, thanks to you, was never grey.

Adieu, my Prince of Pedagogues, adieu!
You, like your coloured chalks, are boxed away.
You taught the Shell what history it knew.
History, thanks to you, was never grey.

Fred Pratt Green: *Ballade of Coloured Chalks*

Return, Alpheus, the dread voice is past
That shrunk thy streams; return, Sicilian Muse,
And call the vales, and bid them hither cast
Their bells and flowerets of a thousand hues.
Ye valleys low, where the mild whispers use
Of shades, and wanton winds, and gushing brooks,
On whose fresh lap the swart star sparely looks,
Throw hither all your quaint enamell'd eyes
That on the green turf suck the honey'd showers
And purple all the ground with vernal flowers.
Bring the rathe primrose that forsaken dies;
The tufted crow-toe, and pale jessamine,
The white pink, and the pansy freak'd with jet,
The glowing violet,
The musk-rose, and the well-attired woodbine,
With cowslips wan that hang the pensive head,
And every flower that sad embroidery wears:
Bid amarantus all his beauty shed,
And daffadillies fill their cups with tears
To strew the laureat hearse where Lycid lies.

Weep no more, woeful shepherds, weep no more,
For Lycidas, your sorrow, is not dead,
Sunk though he be beneath the watery floor;
So sinks the day-star in the ocean-bed,
And yet anon repairs his drooping head
And tricks his beams, and with new-spangled ore
Flames in the forehead of the morning sky:
So Lycidas sunk low, but mounted high
Through the dear might of Him that walk'd the waves;
Where, other groves and other streams along,
With nectar pure his oozy locks he laves,
And hears the unexpressive nuptial song
In the blest kingdoms meek of joy and love.
There entertain him all the saints above
In solemn troops, and sweet societies,
That sing, and singing in their glory move,
And wipe the tears for ever from his eyes.
Now, Lycidas, the shepherds weep no more;
Henceforth thou art the Genius of the shore
In thy large recompense, and shalt be good
To all that wander in that perilous flood.

Thus sang the uncouth swain to the oaks and rills,
While the still morn went out with sandals grey;
He touch'd the tender stops of various quills,
With eager thought warbling his Doric lay:
And now the sun had stretch'd out all the hills,
And now was dropt into the western bay:
At last he rose, and twitch'd his mantle blue:
To-morrow to fresh woods, and pastures new.

John Milton: Extracts from *Lycidas*

Fred in cadet uniform at Rydal

No Gothic palace passing fair,
Whose stately form in mystery fades,
Can ever vie with thee, my school,
Whose stalwart walls for four decades
Have braved the angry northern winds
And laughed to greet the summer days –
Oh! mistress of the storm and calm
Well may Rydalians sing thy praise.

Nature hath wrought thee fairest crown.
There clothed in colour stands the Bryn,
And through the woodland o'er the hill
The sunlit vale of Nant-y-Glyn;
And looming in the distance far
Clouded by haze and rent by storm
With beetling cliffs and sounding caves
Stands as a sentinel, the Orme.

How jocund in thy grounds we wage
The stirring wars of yesteryear,
When round the walls of windy Troy
The men of Corinth hurled the spear:
When Richard of the Lion Heart
Wrought mighty deeds of lasting fame,
Whom all the wild barbaric hosts
In hurtling tumult could not tame.

There in thy courts and on thy fields,
We learn to count the game the prize,
To struggle on when strength is done
And face defeat with steady eyes.
We deem it not a wondrous thing
Thy sons in Flanders beat the foe
For thou hast taught them duty's call,
To be obeyed through weal or woe.

Fred Pratt Green: *Rydal*

Fred's father,
Charles Green

During his Rydal years, Fred gave consideration to pursuing the profession of architect and he maintained an interest in architecture all his life. However, by the time he came to leave school his brother, Osborne, had left Charles Green's leather firm and set up in competition, so Fred joined his father in the family trade. He regarded these years spent in the business world as being of real value in fitting him for his life in the Methodist ministry. They gave him not only a training in the administrative skills useful in church affairs, but also an increased awareness of some of the pressures facing members of his congregations. When negotiating with him in my role as his publisher, I found him financially shrewd but understanding, too, of the needs of those engaged in commerce.

Inevitably there were some communication difficulties between Fred and his father, and these were recalled in his poem *Parents*. But in another text, *Walking with Father*, Fred also acknowledged the inheritance from him of a quick temper, an eye to business and a respect for deity. Other intellectual gifts passed on from Charles Green to his son included a questioning attitude that respected truth more than man-made systems of theology, and skills as a preacher inherited also from another relative from whom Fred derived his second Christian name.

It was the call to the Wesleyan Methodist ministry that led Fred to change direction. On 15 March 1924, he was presented with a copy of the Savoy Edition of Shakespeare's works endorsed 'To dear Mr Fred. A Memento of Many Happy Times. From the Staff, Leather Goods Ltd' followed by eight signatures.

The call had come following a sermon by Rev. William Rushby on John Masefield's poem *The Everlasting Mercy*. Fred was accepted for training at Didsbury College but he first spent a year in the Severn Valley Mission Circuit. His evangelical friends warned him that the College was staffed by 'modernists' in regard to the challenges of Biblical Criticism. As early as 1922 an unidentified friend presented Fred with a copy of a translation of *Marcus Aurelius Antonius to Himself* signed 'from Bill trusting modernity will never spoil your appreciation of Marcus Aurelius Antonius'. It remained by his bedside for the rest of his life as a nightly dip-in book. Fred was at ease as a Methodist minister preaching the centrality of the Gospel of Christ Crucified, while believing that God, in whose image all were created, inevitably communicated part of Supreme Being (or Truth, to put it another way) to all seeking the purpose of human existence. He believed he was the only British Methodist minister at the World Congress of Faiths in 1935. In addition to the annotated copy from Roman days, copies in translation, with his marginal comments, of *The Way of Life according to Laotzu* and *The Ten Principal Upanishads* were among his treasured books.

Fred could therefore sing contentedly these verses from hymn-writer George Matheson, known better for his text *O love that wilt not let me go*:

> Thine is the mystic life great India craves,
> Thine is the Parsee's sin-destroying beam,
> Thine is the Buddhist's rest from tossing waves,
> Thine is the empire of vast China's dream;
> Gather us in.
>
> Thine is the Roman's strength without his pride;
> Thine is the Greek's glad world without its graves;
> Thine is Judea's law with love beside,
> The truth that censures and the grace that saves;
> Gather us in.
>
> Some seek a Father in the heavens above,
> Some ask a human image to adore,
> Some crave a spirit vast as life and love;
> Within Thy mansions we have all and more;
> Gather us in.

Fred would use the word Truth as a synonym for God. More important to him, his Christian beliefs allowed him to use the word Love for his Creator. The final hymn for Fred's funeral service, chosen by him, was Charles Wesley's *Son of God, if thy free grace*.

Before attending theological college, Fred was sent for a year to serve as a non-collegiate minister in the Severn Valley Mission Circuit, which straddled the Welsh Border from north of Oswestry, his father's birthplace, to Welshpool. Fred himself was stationed at Gobowen, not far from Ellesmere where his mother was born.

The chapel at Gobowen is still open today, and the interior is little changed since Fred's time there. His name is on the foundation stone for the school building erected in 1925. In the 1980s, Eddie Jones received a copy of *The Hymns and Ballads of Fred Pratt Green* endorsed 'To my friend Eddie Jones – once a boy in my Junior Choir, Gobowen'. Fred was in correspondence with Eddie as late as 1985, from which date a four-page letter is preserved. Another lad who was a choirboy at Weston Rynn also maintained contact with Fred over the years. He related how, when Fred had an appointment at Craignant Chapel one summer afternoon, a hen from a nearby farm joined the congregation and settled down. During the sermon, the hen made a loud cackling noise, and after laying an egg, fled out through the door, causing a commotion, much to the amusement of all present. I am indebted for this information to Hilda Jones, a fellow-worshipper with Eddie Jones at the Chirk Chapel for many years. Her husband was a miner and served as a lay preacher for 62 years. May Grindley, now in her nineties, also remembers Fred, and Olive Powell of Wrexham remembers hearing Fred preach at Gobowen when visiting friends.

Fred's posting to Gobowen gave him a chance from time to time to tramp his beloved Welsh fells. He could cover as much as 25 miles a day in the roughest terrain.

I've seen so many chapels in Wales
Called by Bible names, beautiful names,
With their windows square as honesty,
Rounded as charity, clear as purity,
I thought He must have come back;
But the deacons all walked with a tread
So solemn, I thought He was dead.

Why, I cried, are the holy chapels
Surrounded by spikes and spears,
And never a flower but the dandelion,
Which I love, mind you, and the singing
Oh beautiful singing but lugubrious,
And the deacons all dressed in black
As if He had never come back?

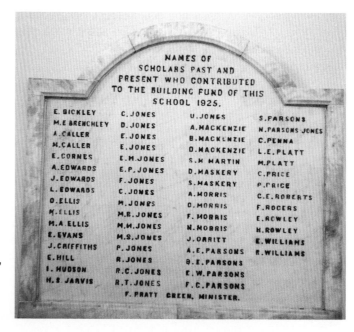

So I passed by the chapels of Wales
Respectfully, mind you, and walked
Where lambs sucked, chaffinches sang,
And lilies of the field were arrayed
Better than Solomon, and the thorn
Flowered, and my heart that had lack
Of Him flowered and put off black.

When I touch my cap to the deacons
They call me by bad names, Bible names,
Such as Backslider, and Son of Belial,
But I go to my own chapel, thank you,
Which has no railings, walls, or windows,
With the singing joyful, and my head
Laughing itself off He isn't dead.

Foundation stone for Gobowen Chapel schoolroom

Fred Pratt Green: *Backslider*

GOBOWEN CHAPEL AND DIDSBURY

And so to Didsbury College at a time when theologians were no longer able to ignore the revelations and insinuations of Biblical Criticism, or ignore the profoundly disturbing findings of the Freudian psychologists or the distressing accusations of Marxist sociology. In their Principal, T. E. Barratt, the students had someone who knew how to handle a generation that included those who had fought in the First World War and were resentful of authority. Two of his fellow students were Francis Westbrook and Douglas Dugard. Both of these were recalled in a poetry cycle *Ten Friends*, written in 1991.

Gobowen Chapel in 2001

DOUGLAS DUGARD

What is it makes someone lovable?
I ask myself this question
as I think of my life-long friend D.D.

Why should hundreds come to your funeral
from far and wide?
You were not a star personality,
or a striking preacher,
or a controversial figure;
you did not distinguish yourself in any sphere,
except in one, yes, except in one.

You had a comfortable, arm-chair presence,
looked lazy, and never did the washing-up;
you were rotund, without being obese;
you exploded easily into laughter
as if life is a great joke.

When we were students at Didsbury College,
with study-bedrooms in Saints' Rest,
we had a hiking holiday in the Lakes.
You were not a three-peaks-in-a-day-man,
or even an eight-miles-in-the-day-man:
but I got you up Helvellyn the easy way.
You suffered from sore feet,
and shortness of breath;
you were not cut out for fell-walking.

Disciplined in the religious life,
you read the best books thoroughly;
you were a catholic nonconformist;
a catholic in your love of worship,
a nonconformist in your love of freedom.
You would have made a good Franciscan.

I suppose you were lovable because you loved:
you loved people, most of all
those you had baptized,
those you had married,
those you had comforted,
those you had buried.
It might be said you never forgot them.

You never aimed at high office,
you had no flair for self-advertisement.
Though you would have looked funny in a mitre,
you had a natural dignity;
you would have made a devoted Pastor Pastorum.

You were always there when most needed.
You would have faced a snowstorm
to save anyone from harm,
and most of us would have died for you.

Your wife had kissed the blarney-stone;
being lovable and supportive,
she helped you to be lovable,
by protecting you from irritants,
by being untiringly hospitable.
You were an entertaining couple
in more senses than one.

Your death was a great shock to us all.
You collapsed at the dinner-table,
and never regained full consciousness.
The world turned out for your funeral.
Your wife did not long survive you.

If there is purgatory,
you will be there for a short time,
doing the washing-up.

Fred Pratt Green: *Ten Friends: D.D.*

Rev. Douglas Dugard (right)
on the occasion of the Greens' Golden Wedding
celebrated at Kirkoswald

FRANCIS WESTBROOK

Of all the people I have known well,
you were the nearest to being a genius.
A shrimp of a man, with a strong face,
and the kind of a voice that can quell
a riot, and a talent for invective,
you had the spirituality of a saint
and a kindliness that made us love you.

Your eccentricity was part of your charm.
I think of you, shambling down the street
vigorously flexing your fingers
in preparation for the next concert.
'I shall walk behind you,' I threatened.
Such a cheerful disregard for custom
amused and embarrassed your friends.

We were at college together. Students
of theology are not the most tolerant;
and to be a genius is to invite trouble.
When you complained of the college pianos,
they tricked you into asking permission
to play a tutor's fretwork-fronted one.
By enjoying the rag you robbed it of venom.

The very thought of being your best man
was intimidating. I swear it is true.
I bought you two pairs of pyjamas
for your honeymoon, emptied a suit-case
of music, disregarding your protest
'I have to go on working for my degree!'
Yet yours was a happy, lasting marriage.

It was natural we should become friends,
you with an ambition to be a composer,
I with an itch to write. Over the years
we had our successes, when your tunes
and my texts made a good marriage.
Sometimes I thought you were too academic.
There were years when we drifted apart.

Your life was music. Why did you decide
to be a minister? It puzzled everyone.
It was said you were obeying the wish
of the mother you adored. I doubt this.
Perhaps it was your innate saintliness.
You lived music. You even looked the part.
Music or ministry? This was your dilemma.

The crisis of loyalty soon surfaced.
It was Anglicanism, not Methodism,
could offer so gifted a musician,
be he priest or layman, the chance,
through self-fulfilment to glorify God.
At times your loyalty seemed quixotic;
it hurt us to see your talents wasted.

But should a saint seek self-fulfilment
except by a rigorous self-denial?
This was Gerard Manley Hopkins' problem.
With your gifts, your intense enthusiasms,
your dedication to the absolute best,
you hoped to make our wildernesses
blossom. You did not fail completely.

Only those of us closest to you
understood your agony of spirit.
When, at last, you left the active ministry,
hoping to find in some other sphere
a way of making music your life,
of being both loyal and self-fulfilled,
we wished you well. In your later years,

when a way was found of using your gifts,
tensions eased, and you had peace of mind.
A living legend, we all honoured you.
One morning, you fainted in church; lying
as if dead, stretched out in the pew,
it was typical of you to insist
on conducting your choir that afternoon.

Fred Pratt Green: *Ten Friends: F.B.W.*

Francis Westbrook's widow tells us that in fact Francis had already gained his degree by the time of their wedding.

Francis Westbrook at the organ of
The Methodist Central Hall, Westminster

FRED AND MUSIC

Part of Mahler's Fourth Symphony was played at Fred's funeral to accompany the Committal

I suppose it is fair to say that I am musical without being either an expert performer or a particularly well-informed listener. Curiously I can improvise on the piano sufficiently well to please myself – and Marjorie. If I tried to do it to an audience, I know I should be too self-conscious to do well. I have to play without thinking very much about it. I may use a phrase and work around it. This sort of 'automatic' playing has no claim to originality: but at least it has a therapeutic value for myself: almost a healing quality: I can work off the unusual black mood this way!

My favourite composers, like my favourite painters, are mostly 'impressionists', especially Debussy, Delius: and of course, the great classical and romantic masters: Mozart, Beethoven, Schubert, and both Mahler and Bruckner. I dislike Richard Strauss and the Wagner operas – in fact, nearly all operas, except the fun operas of Gilbert and Sullivan. Sibelius, of course! Elgar.

A favourite? Mahler's 4th Symphony undoubtedly. I have never forgotten Elisabeth Schwarzkopf singing in the final movement. She, so sophisticated a singer, managed to capture the childlike simplicity Mahler expected.

Of the moderns, most of Stravinsky and some Bartok: most contemporary music I dislike.

In other words, a very conventional listener, for a man of my generation.

Fred Pratt Green: *Diary 1987*

… Maurice Checker, who in the 1950s was a musically talented youth in our Shirley church, and now has his own chamber orchestra in Edinburgh… has discovered a *Carol for Homeless Children (Noël des enfants qui n'ont plus de maisons)*, words and music by Claude Debussy. Written in 1915, the text breathes hatred of the Hun, who has made so many French children homeless. 'Avenge them!' cries Debussy: and the carol ends in a patriotic crescendo. This cannot be sung today, which means that beautiful and dramatic music is unsung. So Maurice asks for a new English text to bring the carol into use. What a marvellous and challenging idea!

The difficulties are considerable. Apart from appeals to Noël (Jesus), the carol isn't Christian: in fact it is anti-Christian in its hatred, despite compassion towards the children. So one has to attempt a radical rewriting of the text, yet keeping the theme of 'homeless children'. Well, there are plenty of homeless children, alas, in our modern world.

The rhythms that sustain a French text are not easily fitted into English. Accents fall wrongly. It would be useful to substitute 'Jesus' for 'Noël' but, except in a few quieter passages, the accentuation is troublesome.

I wrote to Cyril Taylor, sending a First Draft, and of course to Bernard Braley. Useful suggestions were made. It seems that Stainer & Bell are ready to print the revised carol, which Cyril says will flutter the dovecotes. This is more than I dared to hope for! …

I am grateful for such a rare opportunity.

From *Notebook, February 1983*
(Choirs may be interested to know that the setting remains in print.)

You give me music, Lord to compensate
For words that never can express
My utmost joy or intimate distress,
My tenderest love or ill-considered hate.
It fills the place you suddenly vacate,
Or seem to do; it is, in godlessness,
My religion, in loneliness access
To company congenial to my state.

Never to me a drug, or sedative,
Too easy an escape, or ivory tower,
Music, like prayer, relaxes every tension,
Changes my mood, restores a lost dimension,
Gives my small talent new intent to flower.
When you are absent, how else could I live?

Fred Pratt Green: *Music*

Wilfred Calvert, whose name featured in Fred's address book at the time of his death, reveals that his father, Rev. James Knight Calvert, was Superintendent Minister in the Filey Circuit during Fred's time there as a Probationer. His principal role was as Chaplain to Hunmanby Hall School, but also he had pastoral oversight of some village causes and took his place on the Circuit Plan.

The original fireplace in the Dining Hall of Hunmanby Hall School

My memories of Hunmanby in the first year of its existence are very vivid: of Miss Hargreaves (known to us all and forever as 'Harry'), a colourful personality, full of ideas, restlessly energetic; of using the staff room, which meant intruding into a woman's world, and – unconsciously, of course – wondering which of them I liked best; of Sunday worship in the village chapel, which aesthetically left much to be desired (and of trying to persuade village members to vacate the seats they had come to regard as their own in order to place the girls in one block: one old lady refused and for some weeks stuck it out); of the Flamebearer ceremony and of writing a hymn for it, the first and almost only hymn I would write for forty years but presaging my chief occupation in old age; and of teaching while the school was actually being constructed and of giving my famous talk on the Plagues of Egypt while a joiner was finishing off a cupboard (or am I exaggerating?).

continued on next page

THE FLAME

They are almost uniformly happy memories. I had my ups and downs with Harry (who didn't?), but marvelled at the way she managed everyone, including parents, in her determination to give to Hunmanby a tradition worthy of the ideals which inspired the foundation of the school, and to make it a school which would also be a family, a happy family.

In those days, the Chaplain had to teach scripture throughout the school, which in my third year meant seventeen classes a week, as well as to preach on Sundays and look after several village societies. I enjoyed my teaching, though my 'modernism' was occasionally questioned by parents. I doubt if I was always told about it by Harry, who stood by me. Of course, I had my trials.

Some girls were impossible; some girls always are. But some were intelligent and turned in good work. And many were nice. Mind you, teaching girls is much more difficult than teaching boys, simply because you know what boys are up to, girls being less predictable and much more subtle in getting their own way.

Fred Pratt Green: From *The First Chaplain Remembers* in a booklet published in 1978 to commemorate the Golden Jubilee of Hunmanby Hall School

The ceremony itself, which was deeply impressive in its simplicity and spiritual beauty, then followed, commencing with the singing of the hymn:

> O Thou who camest from above,
> The pure celestial fire to impart,
> Kindle a flame of sacred love
> On the mean altar of my heart.

The chaplain lit the lamp from the hearth fire. As the light was kindled for the first time we prayed for the spirit of which we had been thinking.

> O Thou who dwelleth in light unapproachable, and yet whose home is the humble and contrite heart, inspire us at this time with true devotion to Thee and to this school. May the flame of purity, of unselfish love, and of wise adventure burn in us brightly where ever we may be, both now and in the future years, through Jesus Christ our Lord.

The second part of the ceremony was the passing of the flame around the school. All present having their share in the symbolic act. As the light was handed to the Headmistress and then to each group in turn, to the teaching staff, the girls and the household staff, these words were repeated:

> May the spirit of this flame dwell in you, and kindle other hearts.

And so at last the flame returned to the lamp. What must have impressed us all was the quiet reverence which united us all together in our act of dedication and worship. Our ceremony closed with the singing of the hymn written for the occasion. May the inspiration which came to us on that memorable night be re-kindled at every such ceremony, and remain with us forever.

Anonymous. From *The Wood Path*, the School Magazine, Christmas 1928

For many years the Flamebearer hymn, Fred's first, was sung to FOREST GREEN, but in later years a music mistress wrote a new tune which can be found in the book *The Conqueror's Gems*, by Hunmanby pupil and teacher, Genista W. Dawson.

FLAMEBEARERS

God lit a flame in Bethlehem,
O Light! O Living Way!
And every saint who held it high
Was faithful in his day.
And now the splendid torch is ours,
For youthful hands to hold,
That fires once lit in Galilee
May light an English wold.

Thus we would consecrate our hands
To the same shining task,
And call Thy Spirit down on us
And for Thy presence ask.

O may no unlit heart be here,
No feet that miss the Way;
O let no cherished hope be lost,
No bright love ember grey.

Lord! fan Thine ancient Faith in us,
The bearers of the Flame,
That every thought and deed may be
A hallowing of Thy Name;
That in the yet unravelled years
Flamebearers still to be,
Taking the torch from us shall say:
'These, Lord, were true to Thee!'

Fred Pratt Green: *The Flamebearer*

As one of the original pupils of Hunmanby Hall School, I was there when the Rev. Pratt Green was the first school chaplain. He also took Scripture lessons… we were taught to understand the Biblical stories, to appreciate the poetry of the language, and to look for God in nature, especially in the beautiful grounds of the Hall.

Joan Senior's first class ticket

During 1930, the Headmistress gathered in her sitting-room on a Sunday afternoon for preparation classes, those girls who felt ready to become members of the Methodist Church. This culminated in the December, when as we knelt at the communion rail in the old village chapel, the Rev. Pratt Green admitted us into membership and gave us our first communion – a truly wonderful 'special day'!

Schooldays remembered by Joan Senior

I had the good fortune of being one of the original girls at Hunmanby Hall and was there from 1928–1932. Rev F. Pratt Green – or Pratto – was the School Padre from 1928. My memory of him was a friendly approachable person with a good sense of humour. He devised the Lamp Ceremony when a flame from the fire was passed through the whole school at the beginning and end of each school term.

Each Whitsuntide there was a School Open Day for parents and friends. This took the form of a pageant and was accompanied by dancing on the lawn (if it wasn't raining). Pratto wrote these pageants about local history.

As typical school girls we thought he would marry the English mistress: instead in 1931 he married Marjorie Dowsett who taught French and we knew as Dormouse. Pratto took some scripture lessons and at one time he tried to explain away the miracles – not Jesus' healing of people but events like the feeding of the five thousand and changing water into wine at the wedding feast. I found it interesting but other girls were upset and wrote home to their parents. Miss Hargreaves (Headmistress) asked Pratto to stop upsetting the girls in this way.

Over the years I have remained in touch with the Pratt Greens, and later visited him at Cromwell House. Until the last two years Pratto very much enjoyed being taken out to the Maid Marian for lunch when he recalled with amusement his days on the staff at Hunmanby, especially being corrected by Harry.

I never forget my days at Hunmanby Hall and the message: 'May the Spirit of His flame burn in you and kindle other hearts.'

Memories of Pratto contributed by Joan Martin who was awarded an M.B.E. some years earlier for services as a community doctor in North Kensington, to the International Guide movement, and to swimming facilities for the disabled.

Beulah Cottage, Hunmanby, where Fred lodged with Hilda and Joseph Danby from 1928 to 1931.
This old photograph shows Hilda's father and mother, John and Annie Cooper, Hilda herself and her sister.
It was kindly supplied by Trevor Danby.

Fred's extensive partnership with the creative spirit of authors both living and dead provides another clue to the breadth of his own imagination. He was nourished by a wide-ranging diet of literature. Trevor Danby, who was five when Fred moved into his parents' Hunmanby home as a lodger, recalls his room as being filled with books. It was in that same room that Fred wrote his one and only novel, described frankly in his diary in old age.

He asks if I have ever written a novel. The answer is Yes! I wrote a novel called THE WOLDGATE while I lived in Hunmanby (1928–31), much influenced by Thomas Hardy! Bloody awful! I never sent it to a publisher & destroyed it about 10 years later! It was not the kind of novel a Wesleyan Methodist probationer should write!

Fred Pratt Green: *Diary 1987*

When Fred moved to residential care from his home he gave away most of his large library collected over the years, including most of the books he had found useful in his long ministry. Nevertheless, his choice of volumes taken to his bedsit at Cromwell House, and kept on the shelves until his death, provides intriguing insights.

An informal inventory of the surviving titles is presented as a reflection of the wide range of Fred's abiding interests.

Teihard de Chardin: *Le Milieu Divin*, described as the religious meditation that was the accompaniment to *The Phenomenon of Man*, containing the nucleus of the author's scientific ideas. Several passages that Fred found especially significant are marked or underlined.

Thomas à Kempis: *The Imitation of Christ*, with Fred's markings.

Lionel Blue with Jonathan Magonet: *The Blue Guide to the Here and Hereafter*, a collection drawn from the great treasury of Jewish spirituality, from the Old Testament to modern times, with linking passages by Rabbi Lionel Blue.

G. E. Radford: *My Providential Way*. A Biography of Frances Brotherton Westbrook.

The Book of Common Prayer and *Hymns Ancient and Modern*. Received as a gift in 1936.

Arthur Waley (Translator): *Chinese Poems*. Inscribed 'To Derek from Fallon with all good wishes'.

Rudolf Otto (in translation). *The Idea of the Holy*. An Inquiry into the non-rational factor in the idea of the divine and its relation to the rational.

William Shakespeare: *The Sonnets,* and *A Lover's Complaint*. With Fred's annotations on the first twenty-two sonnets.

Harold K. Moulton: *The Challenge of the Concordance*. Some New Testament words studied in depth. Sent by the author with happy remembrances and much gratitude.

Robin A. Leaver, James H. Litton and Carlton R. Young: *Duty and Delight: Routley Remembered*. A Memorial Tribute to Erik Routley (1917–1982).

Chambers's Cookery and Domestic Economy for Young Housewives. Presented to his mother, Hannah Greenwood with best wishes from N. H., 24 October 1887.

Gerald Rendall (Translator): *Marcus Aurelius Antoninus to Himself*. Inscribed 'To Fred from Bill trusting modernity will never spoil your appreciation of Marcus Aurelius Antoninus'. With markings by Fred.

Peter Dunn: *Death of a Scarecrow*. Poems.

The Holy Bible (The Revised Version) 1924 Printing. Battered from a lifetime of use.

Anthony Trollope: *Barchester Towers*.

Rita F. Snowdon (Editor): *People are People*. Signed copy. The anthology included Fred's poem *You can't teach the heart not to stare*.

W. Keble Martin: *The Concise British Flora in Colour*.

H. Westmann (Editor): *Man in his Relationships* edited by H. Westmann. The title was the theme of the tenth Present Question Conference held in 1954. In his preface the editor writes 'fundamentally the problem for modern society seems to lie in the need for communication between the various specialised fields'. The book is a collection of essays by the speakers at the conference.

C. V. Wedgwood (Editor): *New Poems 1965*. A P.E.N. Anthology of Contemporary Poetry. The anthology contains Fred's *The Old Couple*.

David Fountain: *Isaac Watts remembered*. In Fred's notebooks, he describes himself as more a Watts man than a Wesley man.

Sydney Tremayne: *The Rock and the Bird*, a gift from the author in 1955; *The Swans of Berwick*, inscribed 'To Derrick in deep affection from Fallon, this book by a fellow-poet and mutual friend'; *Time and the Wind*; also *The Hardest Freedom*.

Shio Sakanishi (Translator): *The Spirit of the Brush* being the *Outlook of Chinese Painters on Nature from Ancient China to Five Dynasties A.D. 317–960*.

Guy Boas (Editor): *The School Book of Modern Verse*. This includes Fred's poem *The House of Prayer*.

Poems by John Clare. The best edition of the collected works of John Clare was one of Fred's ten choices when asked which books he would take to a desert island. The early poems were written between hard work as an agricultural labourer. The later ones in lucid intervals in a madhouse, to which he had been driven by hard labour, poor health and alcohol.

The Apocrypha, Revised Version.

W. R. Maltby (Editor): *St Paul's Letter to the Philippians*.

Shree Purohit Swāmi and W. B. Yeats (Translators): *The Ten Principal Upanishads* with Fred's hand-written notes on some passages. This was a gift received in 1940.

Dannie Abse: *Poetry Dimension Annual 5*. This includes Fred's poem *The Old Couple*.

Witter Bynner (Translator): *The Way of Life according to Laotzu*. Fred's inscription in the volume, which contains many of his annotations, reads: 'This book had an immense influence on my attitude to life. But see a later translation by Gia Fu Fenke & Jane English.'

J. R. Watson: *Everyman's Book of Victorian Verse* received with the editor's warmest good wishes.

R. S. Thomas: *Laboratories of the Spirit*. The work of an Anglican poet, whom the Methodist Chairman of the East Anglia District, speaking at Fred's funeral, mentioned in his tribute.

Henry Newbolt (Editor): *Poets of the XVII Century*.

Bonamy Dobrée, Louis MacNeice & Philip Larkin: *New Poems 1958*. This contains Fred's poem *Spastics*.

Mary Ingate: *The Sound of the Weir*. Winner of £2,500 Crime Competition. Signed by the author.

Herbert Jenkins: *Patricia Brent, Spinster*. Novel.

The New English Bible. New Testament.

F. T. Palgrave: *The Golden Treasury*. With additional poems. Used at school in 1918.

Brian Frost: *Glastonbury Journey*. Marjorie Milne's search for reconciliation.

Shri Purohit Swāmi: *The Geeta*. Annotated by Fred and inscribed, 'This Book belongs to F. Pratt Green and is exceedingly precious to him'.

Lionel Stevenson & Others (Editors): *Best Poems of 1960*. This includes Fred's *Sonnets for a New Decade* or *Lil and Merle*.

Helen Alexander and Bernard Braley: *Pocket Praise*.

Pears Cyclopaedia 90th Edition. 1981.

Graham Greene: *Monsignor Quixote*.

The Illustrated Gospels with full colour plates. Undated.

Timothy Beaumont (Editor): *Modern Religious Verse*. This includes Fred's *Backslider*.

Braley, Percival & Tillman (Editors): *The Galliard Book of Carols*. Includes several newly written lyrics by Fred Pratt Green.

Hymns and Songs. The supplement to the *Methodist Hymn Book*, 1969.

Peter Dunn: *Flowering Grasses*, inscribed to 'My Dear Derrick, Best and most sensitive of friends and critics, As ever, Peter'.

Maurice Wollman (Editor): *Stories in Modern Verse*. This includes Fred's *Cain's Self-Defence*.

Harold Monro: *Twentieth-Century Poetry*. Published 1929.

Philip Larkin (Editor): *The Oxford Book of Twentieth Century Verse*. This includes Fred's *The Old Couple*.

Lionel Stevenson & others (Editors): *Best Poems of 1968*. This includes Fred's *Portrait of a Stoic*.

William Barnes: *Poems of Rural Life in the Dorset Dialect*, 1909.

Virginia Woolf: *To the Lighthouse*.

The Poetry Society's Verse Speaking Anthology. This contains Fred's *Wiltshire Lane* and *The Ship*.

G. M. Glaskin (Novelist): *A Bird in My Hands*.

The Methodist Service Book. 'Presented with many thanks on the occasion of our wedding from Alfred and Joan'. 14th November, 1981.

F. E. S. Finn: *Voices of Today*. This includes Fred's poem *The Victim Died of Stab Wounds*.

John Wesley: *A Collection of Tunes, set to music, as they are commonly sung at the Foundery*. 1981 Facsimile. (John Wesley's first tune book.)

Rex Warner, Christopher Hassall & Laurie Lee: *New Poems 1954*. A P.E.N. Anthology. This contains Fred's *The Next Minute*.

Peter Porter & Charles Osborne (Editors): *New Poetry*. This includes Fred's *The Death of Mussolini*.

Alan Webster and Sister Wendy: *Julian of Norwich*. An introduction to the *Revelations of Divine Love*.

Lucy M. Owlston: *Hunmanby: East Yorkshire*. A story of ten centuries.

John Wesley: *Collection of Psalms and Hymns*. (Facsimile). 'For Fred Pratt Green with deep appreciation for his many hymns which continue the intention of the missionary priest John Wesley to allow Christians to sing of their own experiences.' Endorsed 'Presented to F.P.G. when the American Youth Choir (Methodist) visited Ely on 22/6/88'.

Roget's Thesaurus. Penguin Edition bought 1982.

Jean and Howard Sergeant: *Poems from Hospital*. This includes Fred's *Spastics*.

J. R. Watson: *The Poetry of Gerard Manley Hopkins*. (Penguin Critical Studies.)

A Free Church Book of Common Prayer, 1929.

Patric Dickinson, J. C. Hall & Erica Marx: *New Poems 1955*. This includes Fred's *After Reading a Book of Ferns*.

Kenneth Clark: *Civilisation*.

Thomas Sheehan: *The First Coming*. How the Kingdom of God became Christianity.

Bernard Braley: *Hymnwriters 1*. Biographies of Ken, Cowper, Heber, How and Ellerton.

Bernard Braley: *Hymnwriters 2*. Biographies of Newton, Montgomery, Baker and Bayly.

Wayne Davies: *Palaces of Europe*.

Rosenthal: *Constable: The Painter and his Landscape*. 'Presented to Reverend Doctor Fred Pratt Green with best wishes by the Directors of Stainer & Bell Limited on the occasion of his eightieth birthday.'

Robert Browning: *The Byzantine Empire*.

Adrian Vincent: *Victorian Watercolours*.

Country Life Picture Book of Britain in Colour. 'Presented to Mrs F. Pratt Green by The Women's Work Committee of Trinity Methodist Church, Sutton in gratitude for her leadership as their President 1964–1969. And with good wishes for a long and happy retirement. 17th July 1969.'

The Times, past, present, future. To celebrate two hundred years of publication.

Hymns Ancient & Modern Revised.

Tim Noble: *Great VS Climbs in the Lake District*.

Willy: *Poems for To-Day, Fifth Series*. 1963. This includes Fred's *Backs to the Engine*.

Chaim Bermant: *The Walled Garden*. The Saga of Jewish Family Life and Tradition.

Edith B. Holden: *Nature Notes for 1906*. Inscribed 'To my dearest Marjorie from her Edwardian husband. December 1978'.

SCRABBLE

Newport: *A Hand and Flower Anthology*. 1980. This includes Fred's *Question and Answer*.
Ernest Gowers (Reviser): *Fowler's Modern English Usage. Second Edition*.
Norman Lebrecht: *The Book of Musical Anecdotes*.
Michael Grant: *History of Rome*.
John Morris: *Londinivm*. London in the Roman Empire.
Maley & Moulding: *Poem into Poem*. This includes Fred's *The Old Couple*.
Julian and her Norwich. Commemorative essays and handbook to the Exhibition 'Revelations of Divine Love', 1973.
AA Illustrated Guide to Britain. 1978 edition.
Heath-Stubbs: *Images of Tomorrow*, 1953. This includes Fred's poem *Question and Answer* and *Slackwater Stillness*.
Michael Wood: *Domesday*. A Search for the Roots of England.
The Guiness Book of Poetry 1959/60. This includes Fred's *Sonnets for a New Decade* or *Lil and Merle*.
Hymns and Psalms. The 1983 Methodist Hymn Book.
James Herriot's Yorkshire.
Alexander Frater: *Great Rivers of the World*.
Shakespeare's Works. The Savoy Edition. Covered engraved F. P. G. 15.3.24. Endorsed 'To dear Mr Fred. A Memento of Many Happy Times. From the Staff, Leather Goods Ltd'.
Gilbert White: *The Natural History of Selborne*. Folio Society Edition. 'Presented to the Rev. F. Pratt Green, the First Chairman of the York and Hull District. He came – a Stranger. He leaves – Beloved. 2nd May 1964.'
The New English Bible. Old and New Testaments.

When Fred and Marjorie moved from their own Norwich home into Cromwell House, the bulk of his library found its way into either The Pratt Green Collection at the University of Durham or on to the bookshelves of others. Further insights into Fred's wide reaching range are revealed in entries selected from his diaries for 1986 and 1987. With so wide a range of literary interests, it is not surprising that Fred was a dab hand at Scrabble; though he found his wife a tough competitor.

Fred playing Scrabble

FRED'S READING CHOICES

Edmund Gosse's 'Father and Son' has been a favourite book since my first reading of it sixty years ago. Now I am reading Ann Thwaites's marvellous biography of Gosse. The fascination of this book lies in the careful checking by the author of the real facts of that extraordinary relationship. She proves that the picture Edmund Gosse drew of his father, long after the years of anguish, exaggerates the severity of Philip Gosse, but faithfully describes the immensely long process by which Edmund at last broke away from a father who loved him passionately. Or perhaps it is more accurate to say that Edmund tends to telescope time, heightening the drama by so doing.

Another genius, if this isn't too grand a word, is also in my thoughts: Christopher Isherwood, whose extraordinary book about himself, 'Christopher and his Kind', is my present bedtime reading. Self-exposure is his business, but done in such a shrewd way one is intrigued and not 'put off' by it. All books about homosexuality and about homosexuals, fascinate me. Years ago, I read E. M. Forster's 'Maurice', about which Isherwood was consulted. Although a mother-fixation is likely to breed homosexuality, there is no evidence that Lowry was one. Or is there? I must see if there's a frank biography available.

The other day someone asked me if I read novels. I replied: yes, but they are not my favourite reading, which is biography, autobiography, and 'pure' history. 'What is your favourite novel?', I was asked.

That question set me thinking. I have a habit of somehow getting interested in a particular novelist and reading a number of his/her books. So I have read round Graham Greene, Antony Powell, Muriel Spark, E. M. Forster, Paul Scott (before 'The Jewel in the Crown'!), and Virginia Woolf.

My favourite novel is definitely her 'To the Lighthouse'. I must have read it four times during the past thirty years and always with a growing appreciation of its subtle characterisation, its unhurried pace, and the sheer poetry of its perceptions and language. It is a kind of poem, but without the purple passages that rather mar – to my way of thinking – the great classical novelists like Thomas Hardy.

Now, I am reading, for the first time, the collection of Virginia Woolf's writings called 'Moments of Being'. I hadn't realized how closely 'To the Lighthouse' is descriptive of her own family life in childhood. Her parents are brought to life in Mr & Mrs Ramsey as 'Moments of Being' reveals – a wonderful study of her beautiful and perceptive mother.

It turned out that I began to talk about two books which greatly influenced me in youth and middle life: 'The Meditations of Marcus Aurelius' and 'The Way of Life (Tao Te Ching) of Lao Tzu'. I read to him the wonderful opening pages of the Meditations, with the great Emperor's list of those to whom he owed the greatest debt: and I expounded Lao Tzu's brand of pacifism. The idea of any inspired wisdom, outside the Christian Scriptures, is always disturbing to evangelicals.

My present library books are: *William Marshal: the Flower of Chivalry* by Georges Duby; *The Man with Two Shadows* by Robin Maugham; *The Cockatoos*, stories by Patrick White; *Evelyn Waugh and his World,* edited by David Pryce-Jones.

A pretty mixed bag. The book on chivalry, based on a medieval poem, is unlike anything I have read. It gives an extraordinary picture of one aspect of the Middle Ages. I have a liking for Robin Maugham and vividly remember 'The Servant'. The current television series on Australia has reminded me that I have never read a Patrick White novel; his shorter stories may be an easy introduction. As for Evelyn Waugh – he and his period fascinate me!

For some years now, I have read little theology and few devotional books. I enjoy light reading, usually detective stories; but really prefer a biography of an author or artist for its psychological interest.

Fred Pratt Green: *Diary 1987*

MARJORIE M. DOWSETT B.A., A.K.C.

Marjorie Mildred Dowsett, known to the pupils at Hunmanby Hall as Dormouse, was the school's first French mistress. Granddaughter of a Peckham sheepskin dresser and daughter of an Eltham master window cleaner, she was born on 30 July 1905. She attended Eltham High School and went on to study French and theology at college.

The girls of Hunmanby Hall reckoned that the chaplain would court the English mistress; but, in the privacy of a Scarborough Methodist Manse, Marjorie was Fred's choice.

Marjorie while at Hunmanby Hall

MARRIAGE

Fred was ordained at the Wesleyan Methodist Conference in 1931. The couple were wed in August of the same year and honeymooned in Venice.

(Left to Right) (2) George Dowsett (3) Hannah Green
(5) The Bridegroom (6) Best Man Eric Thomas (7) The Bride
(8) Charles Green (9) Mrs Dowsett

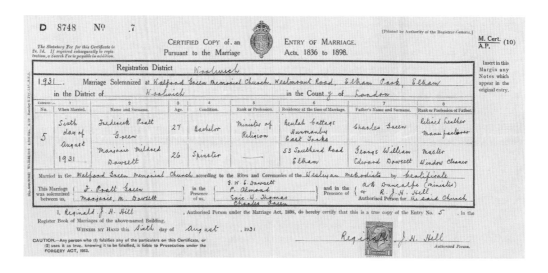

MARJORIE AND DERRY

Marjorie and I have been wed for 56 years! We've had our difficulties, especially in the early years, but nothing has prevented us from loving each other and overcoming our difficulties. These years of retirement, eighteen of them, have been ones of increasing happiness, for many years with Mary (Sister Mary Randall) as a friend sharing our home, but latterly just our two selves.

Marjorie and I are alike in most things: in our religious views, in our attitudes to everyday living (we like much the same kind of food), and especially in our love of the country. Neither of us yearns for summer holidays in Spain, Crete, or Malta (where some of our friends go); we are quite happy to go to the Yorkshire Dales or to the Lakes, or (years ago) to the far north of Scotland. We grumble about the weather, but don't mind all that much!

Of course we also differ. Marjorie is a staunch Conservative, even a Thatcherite; I'm a typical floating voter. Marjorie is likely to be dubbed racist in some of her views (but in any personal relationships entirely friendly: we had African students living with us after the war); I'm pro-Mandela, etc! And in music we are miles apart. She can't even enjoy THE RITE OF SPRING. However, we neither of us like Grand Opera and screeching or wobbling sopranos. I loved the Beatles and now hate violent Rock; she has always disliked 'Pop'. I don't think she really enjoys hymns, but she's a shrewd judge of any I write and therefore very useful to me. She's violently pro FPG, which is sweet of her. I have read this to M and she says it's fine!!

Fred Pratt Green: *Diary 1987*

These verses are from some of Derry's greeting cards to his wife. Derry was Marjorie's pet name for her husband.

1
I chose this Christmas card, my dear,
To bring the magic back
That used to lure us, year by year,
To watch WHITE HEATHER and GOOD CHEER
Make for this harbour before turn of tide;
To taste crab salads and cream teas,
And walk the cliffs to Looe
Through stonechat country in a breeze
That tossed your dress above your knees,
And spread the scents of summer far and wide.

Do you remember how we fled,
as far north as we could,
sensing a slow corruption spread
Vulgarity? No! think instead
How you discovered in a ferny lane
A rarity called BASTARD BALM;
And how in nights of storm
We waited, sleepless with alarm,
For hungry seagulls to confirm
'The fishermen are safe and home again!'

2
All our together life
we have loved flowers:
willow-herb and loosestrife,
comfrey and chicory,
counted umbelliferae
rather specially ours –
Now before petals fall
in our sunniest hours
we know that love survives
beyond our present lives,
the fairest flower of all.

3
Another year! So much to lose or win!
Though so unlike, how well we dove-tail in!
In argument we may be poles apart,
Knowing what each will say before we start,
Yet share the *Daily Telegraph*, and meet
on common ground, in *Coronation Street*.
Here is Woodbastwick, beautiful in snow,
One of the places where we like to go.

4
How many things there are, exotic, rare,
We still remember: breakfasting on grits;
A double rainbow in the London Blitz;
A humming bird that hovered in the air
(Do you remember it? Can you say where?);
Orchids in Bradford; snow in early June
On Lakeland fells; a singer and a tune
In Tenerife (alas, you were not there!)

5
My love, to mark your eighty-second year
I offer you this nice old-fashioned card
Of bluebell woods, a homely souvenir
Of all the simple pleasures we have shared.
As we grow old in love is it not clear
Things most familiar to us are most dear?

6
One day Old Age confessed
Times past were best;
But God replied:
I was born and died
For Tomorrow.
Therefore, without fear or sorrow,
Step out, dear Love, with me
Into Eternity.

MARJORIE'S LIFE AND MINISTRY

The customs of the twenties were such that wives were not expected to undertake paid employment on their own account. Marjorie was unwavering in her loyal support of her husband, but after her brief professional life as a schoolmistress she remained very much her own person. This daughter of a London window cleaner was a fine theologian, who shared insights, quite distinct from those of her marriage partner, with many church groups. Many remember her as a person with a great sense of fun. Rich friendships grew, several of which lasted till death.

One particular association, which began while the Greens were resident at Grange Park in the 1940s, was with Nora Shepherd. She was married to Rev. Vincent Shepherd, a missionary in Burma at the time of the Japanese invasion, who escaped to India. The daughter of the marriage, a lively and precocious child, lived with her mother in nearby Winchmore Hill. When Nora learned that her husband, suffering from leprosy, was in Vellore Christian Medical Hospital as a likely long-stay patient, she wished to go to South India to be with him. So for about six years the Greens, who had no children of their own, were to act *in loco parentis* to Beth. Although Elizabeth was away at boarding school in term time, in a very real sense, the Greens gained a daughter and Elizabeth a second mother and father during the vital adolescent years. Eventually, the Shepherds were able to return to England, but died a few years later.

When the Greens retired to Norwich, Marjorie used her linguistic skills and theological understanding to become one of the corps of guides at Norwich Cathedral, a service she was able to continue well into her eighties.

Photograph of an original painting, by Owen Waters, which hung in the Greens'
Norwich Home. This painting was especially appreciated by Marjorie.

POOL-IN-WHARFEDALE

Fred and Marjorie moved to Pool-in-Wharfedale in Methodism's Otley Circuit in West Yorkshire on returning from their honeymoon in 1931. As well as gaining their newly ordained minister, the circuit received a fully accredited local preacher in Marjorie.

Methodism began in Pool-in-Wharfedale within the Otley Circuit when the dwelling of James Thompson was licensed in 1796 for Methodist preachings. In 1839, part of a cottage garden was sold for £15 by Michael Nicholson, a paper manufacturer, to fifteen trustees. Three of them were local men, described as a 'paper maker', a 'labourer' and a 'cornwainer'. Seventy years later, in 1909, the village was growing and the then existing chapel was hidden away in a cul-de-sac. The present chapel was built on land given by the Atkinson family. The chapel today owes much for its buildings, furnishings, ornamentation and music to the Atkinson, Whiteley and Reed families.

Members of the Whiteley family (sitting in the three left hand places in the front row) at the 50th anniversary celebrations in 1959

BACKGROUND TO THE BEGINNING OF FRED'S ORDAINED MINISTRY

This new beginning for the Greens was at a time of serious national crisis. The nation was bankrupt. At the end of July, the Economy Committee had recommended salary cuts for the armed forces, teachers and police, a reduction in unemployment pay, substantial tax increases and wide-reaching economies in many other directions. On 24 August, newspapers reported the demise of the Labour government and the formation of a government of co-operation. The small new cabinet had four Labour, four Conservative and two Liberal members. Ramsay MacDonald continued as Prime Minister but was denounced by most Labour members of parliament as a traitor to his party. Unemployment levels were rising towards the three million mark. In September, the gold standard was abandoned and the pound devalued from $4.86 to $3.40. There was unrest in the armed services, with some pay cuts as high as 25%: 12,000 sailors staged what the press called a mutiny. Ships were prevented from sailing for two days. Strikes spread across the country and there were riots in some major cities.

A general election ensued on 28 October, with 554 M.P.'s (including 473 Conservatives) supporting the National Government and 56 (including 52 Labour members) opposed to it. A 100% duty was imposed on all imports, following a bill rushed through parliament. A world economic summit met in 1933, but failed to reach agreement on a solution. Mass unemployment and severe poverty continued. In January 1934, the price of butter was the lowest in living memory. In March 1934, farmers appealed to the government for help as the price of eggs dropped to the lowest level since 1914.

Fred's years in the Otley Circuit also saw Adolf Hitler take over as Chancellor of the German Reich, and widespread civil disobedience in India, to mention only two world events.

A drawing of the church today, by Jean Beever, the wife of the present church organist

Fred mentions in his memoirs that at the time of his arrival in Pool, the society was benevolently dominated by the Whiteleys, owners of the paper mill. It was the Whiteleys who made it possible to have a resident minister in Pool from 1927 and a manse in 1931. So it was to a newly furnished home, *Hazel Lea*, that Fred brought his bride. Today, it would hardly be worth mentioning that he brought a wife with a university degree. Then, however, it was rare. Marjorie not only had a B.A. with Third Class Honours in French, but had also been elected as an Associate of King's College London following examinations in divinity. Fred had six village causes in his care. He was blessed with a superintendent minister who was a fine gentleman and a very good friend, for whom the traditional frock coat and silk hat of the ministry had only recently gone out of fashion.

In December 1933 the new *Methodist Hymn-Book* was published. In 1929, the Conferences of the branches of Methodism contemplating union had set up a joint committee to undertake the work. Many Wesleyans, Fred notes, severely criticised it for having too many chorus-hymns, beloved by Primitives, and other 'inferior' material. He comments wryly that every new hymn-book is opposed. The fiercest radicals in every other walk of life are fiercely conservative when it comes to hymns and liturgies. The book was to serve Methodism for the next fifty years.

I think it must be from this period that Fred's story of a cancelled Harvest Festival arose. The farmers in one village, after a very bad harvest, told their minister that the Harvest Festival must be cancelled: there was no harvest to celebrate. It was duly cancelled. A few weeks later, the farmers relented, saying that all in all there were blessings to be counted. The belated harvest celebration took place.

Returning to Pool in 1959 for the fiftieth chapel anniversary, Fred told of his first service at North Rigton that, when he announced the collection, the steward said, 'Nay lad we don't take collection in't morning.' Then four newcomers, strangers, joined the congregation. The steward gave a knowing wink and said, 'Tha's forgotten the collection, lad', and said on the side 'We allus takes it when we've visitors.'

MASS UNEMPLOYMENT AND WAR CLOUDS

A Few Events in the British and World Calendar during the Girlington Years

16 September 1934: Munich Lutherans march in a demonstration against Adolf Hitler, singing anti-Nazi songs.

5 October 1934: Russian bell-ringers, choristers and churchwardens, but not priests, are allowed to vote in Soviet elections.

4 December 1934: Third-class return railway fares are reduced in Britain to a penny a mile.

18 March 1935: A thirty-mile-an-hour speed limit is introduced in built-up areas in Britain.

18 June 1935: The Japanese win a bloodless victory in Manchuria when the Nationalist Government of China accedes to their demands.

15 August 1935: German–Jewish marriages are banned by Hitler.

16 November 1935: Tories win the British general election.

7 March 1936: German troops enter Rhineland.

8 April 1936: Mussolini uses mustard gas in Abyssinia.

27 May 1936: *Queen Mary* sails on her maiden voyage.

5 October 1936: The Jarrow unemployed begin their march to London.

12 December 1936: King Edward VIII abdicates.

12 May 1937: King George VI and Queen Elizabeth are crowned.

28 May 1937: Neville Chamberlain becomes Prime Minister.

1 August 1937: Concentration Camp opens at Buchenwald.

18 March 1938: Cheering crowds greet Hitler's troops as Austria is annexed by Germany.

3 July 1938: Railway locomotive *Mallard* makes history by travelling at 126mph.

30 September 1938: The Prime Minister returns from Munich promising 'Peace for our time'.

5 October 1938: German troops march into the Sudetenland.

3 March 1939: German troops enter Prague.

31 March 1939: Chamberlain pledges to defend Poland.

5 April 1939: Plans are announced to evacuate two-and-a-half million children should war break out.

31 August 1939: Evacuation of children from London and other cities begins.

In September 1934, Fred moved to the then Bradford (Manningham) Circuit, with pastoral responsibility for the church at Girlington. Unlike the society at Pool, which is still very much alive, Fred's second church as an ordained minister closed around the time the present Pool chapel building celebrated its fiftieth birthday.

Although traditions were changing at Girlington, it was still true that social status determined patterns of seating at morning worship: a rising status meant promotion downstairs from the gallery to the main area. Fred was deeply disturbed by the great divide between the financially better-off and those from the rows of back-to-back houses; and he preached at his first Harvest Festival to his poor-and-affluent congregation that God had provided the produce of the earth for the benefit of everyone.

On Sunday afternoons, besides Sunday School for about 100 children in each age group, there were also a 40-strong Men's Class and a Women's Class of similar size. Fred himself led and built up the Young People's Class. Those in their late teens when he arrived remember him with great affection. He was delighted to preside at some of their weddings. Fred also took part in the wide spread of weekday activities including the Cricket and Tennis Clubs, a Men's Institute with two full-size billiard tables, and the Wesley Guild.

Muriel Robinson, widow of Methodist minister Wilfred Robinson, lived before her marriage in a house opposite the manse, and remembers the Greens visiting for meals. She also kept an eye on their house if they were away. Both Muriel and her mother were members of the Drama Group and both performed in *The House at Arrow Ghyll,* which Fred wrote for their use. She also recalls pageants that he devised.

GIRLINGTON

The dramatic talents of Girlington Methodist Church under Fred's direction

Allen Percival, sometime Principal of the Guildhall School of Music and Drama and later Executive Chairman of Fred's publishers, Stainer & Bell Ltd, was born in Girlington. Though a non-Methodist, he attended the Girlington Youth Club, which he said was the best in the area. Allen wrote settings and arrangements of folk tunes for Fred's words in *The Galliard Book of Carols*. Here follows a letter he sent to Fred following his second marriage in 1990.

Dear Fred, Greetings! We thought you might like to see the enclosed on my marriage Service of Blessing, since so many who were there enjoyed singing your hymn and voices were raised even from your Bradford past. You may or may not remember that I was born in Girlington: my wife Margaret's uncle Tom Robinson was a strong member of your congregation there! Rachel died three years ago and I re-met Margaret a year ago (and a bit). We had known each other as children in Bradford when her father, Donald Brook, was a Methodist minister. She had been unhappily married for many years (whereas I had been totally happy with Rachel). Amazingly, and we are sure with Divine agreement, we are devoted...and in love.

Margaret's divorce was quick and she has found herself on better terms with her 'ex-' ever than she was in their marriage. I get on, too, with all her family very well, particularly her brother Donald (who was at Bradford Grammar School with me!). It is all like playing out a beautifully-constructed romantic novel but the 250 friends who came to the Service of Blessing know that it is real. I am sorry to hear from Bernard that your wife is not too well (also from a talk with Gordon Barritt after service last Sunday at Wesley's Chapel) and hope that you both nevertheless get some joy from life. Thank you for writing the Blessing hymn: it meant a great deal. With all good wishes. Yours sincerely, Allen.

There immediately follows on the same piece of paper:

Dear Fred, I remember you <u>so</u> well as that minister who was such a marvellous preacher! And I remember your black hair smoothed back so smartly. These are teenage memories. I cannot tell you how much your words have meant to us. Our friends are <u>so</u> impressed (few of them Methodists). Our organist, a music therapist I trained in 1976, thinks all weddings should include your hymn. We have given Paul Hulme the two copies of your hymns and ballads. I <u>do</u> so hope we can meet ere long. Yours in His Love, Margaret (Brook!)

The church at Girlington closed towards the end of the 1950s. Today this is an area of Bradford with a large Asian population.

FRED AS PLAYWRIGHT

This is a convenient point to include a survey of Fred's creativity in the field of drama.

Very few people realise that Fred Pratt Green wrote at least thirteen plays. These plays fall into three groups: the early period 1928–1930; the middle period 1930s–1940s; the late period 1970s. Each period has its peculiar characteristics. *Farley Goes Out, Emancipation,* and *Sons of Daybreak Street*, are unashamedly missionary plays, serving the purpose for which they were written: to make the audience face what Christianity means in reality. For example, in both *Farley* and *Sons of Daybreak Street* the call to serve on the mission field is in contrast to the prosperity and university education enjoyed by the two young men who abandon wealth and position, not what their families had wanted for their sons. *Emancipation*, whose time-span covers a century, deals not with personal relationships but with the long-term commitment the Church must make when it embarks on missionary work, indicating that in 1834 the day of emancipation was the beginning, not the end.

The 1930s plays present social and moral issues and dilemmas. *The Skyfarer, The House at Arrow Ghyll*, and *The Night is Dark*, were published by the Lampas Press, as was *The Tree of Peace* (it is hoped that a copy of this play may one day be found). *The Skyfarer* considers the ethical implications of making money from arms' manufacturing. *The House at Arrow Ghyll* is about the need for self-knowledge, a theme continued in *The Night is Dark*. Other plays from this period are *Left Luggage*, a comedy, known only because it is advertised on the cover of *The Skyfarer* but for which, as yet, no text has been found, and *Nursery Farm*, a play for children, which includes 'songs that the children of England sang when England was young' (from the Foreword by Fred Pratt Green). The copyright date of 1939 suggests this play may be the last pre-war play, written just before the Greens left Bradford, severing links with the Lampas Press.

In 1946 the Methodist Youth Department published *Plane from Basra*. Acutely aware of the political situation in the Middle East, Pratt Green wrote of this play: 'it is intended to give audiences something to think about as well as an evening's entertainment.' He portrays a post-war society where all is changed: the role of woman, the role of Christianity now one of several faiths, rather than the main faith; the price paid in human terms for progress; the effect on Muslim society as it absorbs ideas from other cultures. In its construction, understanding and mirroring of post-war society, this forms a bridge to the late plays.

These late plays were never published; they were written for the Helm Players in Norwich. *A Kind of Resurrection, The Star of Peace* and *Red for Danger* were all performed locally with great success. It is impossible to do justice to these three-act plays within these confines. *A Kind of Resurrection* has resonance for today because of hostages like Terry Waite; *The Star of Peace* is a liturgical and symbolic play, while *Red for Danger* is less human and more schematized into a Christian versus godless state, raising the question of how much force should be used against force.

These last plays adopt styles and techniques not found in earlier plays. All use parallels, symbolism, and levels of meaning. For example *A Kind of Resurrection* (Fred's Easter message in dramatic form) uses panelled cupboards representing darkness, death, the tomb, the recesses of the mind, while *The Star of Peace* uses contrast and imitative action of characters, with different levels of staging, to make the audience think beyond the usual nativity scene. In earlier plays the stage directions were brief. Here they are added carefully, deliberately. What Pratt Green is doing is to use drama as a vehicle for pointing us towards recognizing truth about ourselves, our actions and Christian beliefs.

Maureen Harris: *Drama*

Maureen Harris researched Fred's plays as part of work for her doctorate.

Shortly before 6am on Friday 1 September 1939, the first day of Fred's ministry at Gants Hill, a German army of more than a million men invaded Poland. The British Government had promised to go to Poland's aid if the Germans attacked, though as a country we were ill-prepared for war. In practical terms, there was little which could be done to help the Poles. From 31 August, there had been a mass evacuation of children from London. Hundreds of trains delivered hundreds of thousands of youngsters, each carrying a small suitcase and a gas mask, to myriad unknown destinations. It was the largest mass movement of children in the nation's history. And so it was that a church with a Sunday School of 800 children was almost as childless as the streets of Hamelin after the Pied Piper's visit.

An immediate Luftwaffe air attack on London was expected when, with France, the British declared war on Germany on Sunday 3 September. A universal black-out was ordered. An immediate land blitzkrieg was expected against France. America was quick to announce its intention to remain neutral in the conflict. Call-up notices went out to conscripts. Britain and France made a solemn declaration that they would avoid bombing civilians and did not intend to use poison gas or germ warfare.

Rev. A. Richard Boggis had arrived in Fred's new Circuit a year earlier and they were colleagues until 1941. He writes:

I was appointed after ordination in 1938 to the Grenfell Hall, Romford, with Other Denominations Chaplaincy service to the R.A.F. Station at Hornchurch, during the Battle of Britain days. My first wife and I lived for some months under the Church – which the Local Authority had re-inforced and protected in order to use it as a public shelter for bombed-out people.

Fred soon became a local air-raid warden, eventually being placed in charge of a post manned by thirty wardens. The Thames, the estuary which the black-out could not hide, was only three miles away and was a regular route for the bombers that from September 1940 were to attack London's docks, railways and factories. Civilian casualties were inevitable and the post was kept busy.

Although various church activities continued throughout the war for Fred, both in his preaching and pastoral ministry, there were new needs to be met and new people among whom to meet them. There was the opportunity to serve many who would normally be outside a Methodist minister's sphere of influence. It was a ministry for which this extraordinary, ordinary man had the necessary compassion to weep genuine tears with the devastated and to identify with the curious sense of humour which kept many going through the long, lonely, anxious years in London from September 1939 to August 1944.

Photograph from Girlington days of one of the several historical and missionary pageants staged by Fred during his ministry

INCANTATION IN HONOUR OF THE DEAD

When Fred started to write poetry a few years later he remembered the war dead, including victims of the Spanish Civil War of 1936–9, in his poem *Incantation in Honour of the Dead*:

Walking the shabby streets
I have met them
Walking the waste places
I have met them
Walking the wrangling world
I have met them
Walking among these ruins, how can I forget them?

They were flogged in the streets, dragged to the sealed chamber
They were shot turning a corner of a street in Spain
It was a long time ago
They were indexed for death, drew the unlucky number
They fled down roads to freedom, were shamelessly slain
It was a long time ago
We were too late to save them, if we forget they will not know.

They perished in fire, falling, between cloud and stubble
They mingled their blood freely with all tides that flow
We can do nothing for them
They were buried deeper than hope in the smoking rubble
They sank down and were sealed in the chambers of the snow
We can do nothing for them
They are earth, water, air, gone back to the mother who bore them.

They were slain by the foe-in-the-flesh in the weaponless battle
They were crushed in the steel vice of the smitten air
Does it matter now?
They died in the jungle and desert, on the bright atoll
They died (O my friend!) who knows how, who knows where?
Does it matter now?
Who shall tell us, O who shall tell us how great is the debt we owe?

Walking the shabby streets
I meet them
Walking the waste places
I meet them
Walking the wrangling world
I meet them
Here in these ruins I remember them, I greet them.

Fred Pratt Green: *Incantation in Honour of the Dead*

In September 1944, Fred moved to Grange Park and Oakwood in the London Finsbury Park Circuit. Grange Park was a typical prosperous outer London Methodist suburban church with a range of uniformed organisations for young people, and a programme for all ages. The members included the Lucas family, long-time Methodists. Ray's mother's ancestors had been largely responsible for the setting up of one of the Finchley churches, with the first nucleus gathering in the Thomas' front room.

The invasion of Europe had begun in June: not too many V-1s, the Germans' pilotless rocket–aircraft, reached the outer North London suburb, and most of the 100–150 weapons each day fell further south. In the first month of the V-1 onslaught on London and South-East England over 2,700 bombs killed as many people: 8,000 others were casualties. On 9 September, the first V-2 rocket hit London. In November, lights were switched on in Central London after five years of black-out. On 14 February, 1945, in a day and a night of air bombardment, Dresden was reduced to a smoking ruin. Estimates of the number killed varied between 60,000 and twice that figure: some have placed total casualties as high as 400,000. Total war was indeed the order of the day. War in the West ended in May 1945, and Ray Lucas, then in his teens, got to know Fred. It was the beginning of a friendship between old and young that flourished for the rest of Fred's life.

The poem *R.L.*, one of those in the set *Ten Friends* completed in 1991, describes Ray. Incidentally, it was Ray Lucas, just after it was possible for ordinary citizens to nominate persons to be considered for national honours, who took the initiative in contacting others which led to Fred's award of the M.B.E.

Fred with Ray Lucas and his wife after the Investiture in 1994

RAY LUCAS

When war in the West was over,
and peace established for ever,
with not a cloud in the sky,
we got out our bikes, you and I,
and free from the risk of arrest
spent the day in Epping Forest.

'That was my brother,' you say,
'not me!' Have it your own way!
But here's a photo to show
a bike and a boy you know
mending a puncture, and who
is standing there, watching you?

How old were you then? Fourteen?
a kind of betwixt and between,
a tricky, rebellious season
when even home is a prison,
but not, I can swear, in your case,
with your frank, unclouded face.

You grew up as we expected;
friendly, hard-working, respected,
successful, a family man,
a likeable good Samaritan,
who could even afford to live
as a Bramhall executive.

Sometimes, when you came to Norfolk
to visit the Broads for a week
with youngsters who needed a break,
not only for old time's sake,
or with kindness that condescends,
you came to see us, your friends.

The blow, when it fell, was cruel.
Trade slumped; there was no renewal
of employment. Made redundant,
your life collapsed like a tent
in a gale. What staggers us still
is your guts – call it what you will.

What you did, in spite of advice,
was to buy at the right price
a Post Office so run down
they went to a neighbouring town
if they wanted a stamp – a joke
estate agents didn't invoke!

So goodbye to the company car,
to the best hotels (if they are!):
you had to be up at five
to get out the papers, contrive
to balance the books at night,
and be fit for the uphill fight.

You did it by sweat of your brow,
and long-acquired knowledge of how
to give customers, with a smile,
what they want, make it worth while
to drive from the neighbouring town
to shop in the store you now own.

Not for long! You sold it one day,
at a profit sufficient to pay
for a P.O. of great potential
(if it sold whatever's essential
in that classier neighbourhood).
You were back where you once stood.

Did I catch the word 'retire'?
Impossible! You'll acquire
something else to keep you busy–
not in Bramhall, I'll guarantee!
But wherever it is, please come
to see us, and no one more welcome!

Fred Pratt Green: *Ten Friends: R.L.*

FALLON WEBB

While at Grange Park, Fred made a pastoral call on the family of one of the members of the Sunday School and met the person he later described as the fourth of those especially benign influences in his life. Mother first, then Eric Thomas, schoolboy, A. G. Watt, school master, and now Fallon Webb, a gentle agnostic poet crippled by arthritis. So a friendship began which lasted for two decades and is described in the poem *Ten Friends: F.W.*

The encounter woke the poetry dormant within Fred; and in Fallon Webb he had found a wise tutor and friend to encourage the muse.

To each of my friends I owe a special debt;
What I owe to you is beyond belief.
Yet all the years of our friendship
you were a cripple in a wheel-chair,
to whom a little less pain was a relief.

Our meeting was nearly a non-event.
I had a reasonably good excuse
for not paying that pastoral call.
Was it chance? Was it providential?
Why argue about it? What's the use?

You were not the kind of invalid
my experience taught me to expect;
you made no apology, no fuss.
You took it for granted I understood;
you had no secret pride to protect.

The problem is to find common ground,
to break down the barriers of reserve.
The Selected Poems of T. S. Eliot
happened to be beside you, open
at *The Waste Land*. It needed nerve

to start with that! What wonderful luck!
We cut out all the preliminaries
and got down at once to poetry.
The subject brought colour to your cheeks.
Soon I discovered, to my surprise,

you were that much admired phenomenon
'a published poet'. In my young days
I had written some melancholy verse
in the manner of John Drinkwater.
It was merely an adolescent phase.

In our first meeting you taught me
to find my way through *The Waste Land*.
Only when pressed did you share with me
your own verse. It was introspective.
One poem was entitled *Ampersand*.

I made polite noises. Another day,
I would come to admire that dry tone,
that rejection of sentimentality
in favour of truth, a formal beauty
my Georgian poets had never known.

I stood at the door, saying good-bye.
It was then you made a suggestion:
'Why not each of us write a poem?'
You said we could learn from each other;
to refuse was out of the question.

I cheated, having written a poem,
a one-off, on a holiday in Lakeland
the previous year. Yours was a sonnet
on Judas Iscariot. We agreed
not to pull our punches, as they say.

Every meeting became a workshop.
I recollect daring to call
in question your stress on technique;
you disapproved of my prosiness.
Once when we discussed the magical

in poetry, you pleaded the danger
of consciously striving to achieve it.
'It's a gift from God,' you said.
You could laugh at yourself. 'Sometimes,'
you confessed, 'I want to believe it.'

Soon I began, secretly at first
to submit poems for publication;
then to share the excitement of success,
the gloom of rejection. Poetry,
after all, was only a recreation.

When I moved to Brighton, we kept up
our exchange of poems. It was there
I met P.D. and several others
of our kind. We counted you one of us,
and took our problems to your wheel-chair.

Without you, would I have discovered
a second vocation, and a third?
You lived long enough to receive
hymns instead of poems. I know which,
in your heart of hearts, you preferred.

Fred Pratt Green: *Ten Friends: F.W.*
P.D. in the poem refers to Peter Dunn

ELIZABETH SHEPHERD

Beth

My shadow in this evening light
Is tall and thin: a lanky giant
Striding beside me brisk and buoyant,
Whose contours' bold simplicity
Hints at no complexity
Of character or inward night
Of doubt. Surely it's no illusion,
This air of artlessness in motion?

How different was the shape that tangled
My feet six hours ago: a dwarf
Guilefully jigging across the turf,
Squat, sardonic! And there are others,
Diverse, unlike these, yet their brothers,
That to the incidence of angled
Geometry of sun and earth
Owe the phenomenon of birth.

So are the selves that I project –
Conditioned by fate's time and places –
On those I meet: the varied faces
Of personality that stress
Each its own partial truth and thus
Conceal the whole that none suspect:
The self entire, whose faith resolves
The conflict of constituent selves.

Fallon Webb: *Personae*

My parents, Nora and Vincent Shepherd, were Methodist missionaries in Burma. My father had been a missionary there since 1922. I was born in London, but went to Burma as a new-born, and returned to England when I was in my fifth year. In 1943 my father was in India when he discovered he had contracted leprosy and was treated for three years at Lady Willingdon Leprosy Sanitorium. At this time my mother and I were living in Winchmore Hill with her mother and in September 1944 Marjorie and Derrick arrived in the same circuit at 'The Church in the Orchard' at Grange Park. Marjorie and my mother had become friends through various Women's Work Committees, and in this terrible crisis Marjorie became my mother's confidante as my mother worried about my father, about whether she could, and should, join him in India after his transfer to the Vellore Christian Medical Hospital, and then, what would happen to me.

It was finally decided to send me to Trinity School for Girls in Southport, a boarding school for the daughters of Methodist ministers, and Marjorie and Derrick agreed to become my Guardians, and have me live with them during the school holidays. At this time, I knew 'Auntie Marjorie' quite well, and loved her because she was such fun and we would have 'romps' together. 'Uncle Derrick' was more of an unknown quantity, very intriguing to me. I was 10 years old – I became the Child they did not have till then.

1946: I was devastated by losing my mother, but soon warmed to the welcome they gave me at 12 The Chine. The atmosphere in their home was freer and easier than I was used to. Derrick seemed very glamorous to me (I had not seen my own father since I was 7) and I immediately noticed there was as much eastern philosophy on his bookshelves as western theology, and of course tons of poetry. I used to love listening to him playing the piano, and the fact that he was a poet too made him very special. When we moved to Brighton, and he preached at the Dome, I was thrilled to bits!

continued on next page

ELIZABETH AND THE GREENS

I was with them until I was nearly 16 – formative years. Such a situation has an inbuilt emotional dilemma: how to NOT become too emotionally attached. When my parents came back in 1952, my father now cured of leprosy, I did not want to leave Marjorie and Derrick, I was torn apart again. It was awful for all of us. But M & D had changed my life in an essential way. When my parents left me, I was going to be a missionary doctor – they came back to an Actress! I have Marjorie and Derrick to thank for recognising my gift, enjoying it, and encouraging me to believe I could succeed in this vocation. My parents had churches in Newton Abbot and Bridgend before retiring to London. My mother died in 1965, I emigrated to America, and my father died in 1967. Since then the love between me and Derrick and Marjorie deepened and developed into a true family bond. I visited them over the years even though I was living mostly in North America, and Edmund was as if their grandson. The second essential blessing they brought into my life was their non-judgemental acceptance of who I am, and their seal of approval. This I needed most desperately, because I had broken the sexual rules before my parents died, by leaving my first husband and bearing Edmund out of wedlock. This was so unbearable to my parents, who were wonderful people, but strict in their beliefs about morality, that they said it was 'worse than leprosy'. This was a heavy load of guilt for me to bear, as they died before we could fully reconcile and complete the conversation. Marjorie's and Derrick's understanding, compassion, and concern for my well-being did much to salve and help to heal that wound (see the poem Derrick wrote to me in response to my sending them my own quite frank poetry).

Elizabeth Shepherd

Better not to see you
Better not to have to stand, untouched, within arm's reach
To have to restrain from kissing even the nape of your neck
To refrain from searching your eyes
Or asking too many questions
While we talk smilingly of your career, or dubiously of mine
Better to avoid my reluctance at your leaving
The disintegration of my flesh watching you drive away
Better not to let you see me
Pale like an etiolated plant locked up in a cupboard
Unable to gain its colours from the sun
Better to keep hidden the embarrassment of left over love
To put out of mind the newly purchased silken underwear
Better not to catch at glimpses
Better not even to phone

Elizabeth Shepherd: *November in Hollywood*

Greetings Card (words right)

A yellow packet from California!
Holy angels! our Elizabeth has turned poet!
As one poet to another,

as winetasters assess
the year's vintage, I savour your words,
their bitter sweetness.

How the pages crackle
with the inexhaustible, irresistible energy
of your loving! Darling,

do you still offer your body
as love's instrument, do you still wait
for a virtuoso to play

on it with skilled fingers?
Was it the last, the French boy, who did it best?
Reading between the lines

of 'November in Hollywood',
he has gone. Has your 'disintegrated flesh'
returned to form in the fire

of a new love? Counting you
(the child you once were, the woman you are)
our own, we are touched

that you trust us not to be shocked.
Why should you we be when He is not? Always
he warmed towards those

who loved much. So, if need be,
wear it, the flower of Christ's compassion,
Elizabeth, in your bright hair.

Fred Pratt Green: *To Elizabeth – with Love*

Darling Two
A girl needed a father and mother
A pair with no child said they'd love her
since that long time ago
Increasingly so
They have all three adopted each other
Love you – Elizabeth

BRIGHTON

Beth had a considerable impact on the Greens' life during their Brighton ministry. Although resident with them only during the school holidays, this lively and precocious child brought a great joy to their marriage. Marjorie and Fred treated their *in loco parentis* role conscientiously and, realising she had neither the will or talent to become a medical missionary, supported her in her determination to become an actress. This extract is from Fred's diary in 1987 during a visit from her son Edmund, and it begins by recalling the Brighton days.

...And she was exhibiting all the gifts, even including a temperament. We stood by her at this critical time, and she did become an actress. Immediately after a drama course at Bristol University, and an inter-varsity drama competition, in which she won the prize for the best female, got an important part with Andrew Cruickshank in a West End production... Edmund is the sort of son-we-never-had and while we rarely see him – he lives in New York and is training to be an architect – he is always welcome.

Fred Pratt Green: *Diary 1987*

Fred followed Elizabeth's subsequent acting career with the concern of a doting but not uncritical 'parent'. He reflects that she has always had the talent for stardom but has lacked the wisdom to know how to play her cards. 'Give Beth her due: she wanted to play in the great plays, old and new, rather than inferior plays and films.' She spent part of her career doing this with the Canadian Shakespeare Company and secured at least local fame for her fine performances as Katherine of Aragon and Lady Macbeth.

Above: Sunday Evening Worship at the Dome
Left: The Dome Concert Hall, Brighton

PETER DUNN

In 1947 Fred was transferred from his work at Grange Park to the troubled Dome Mission Circuit in Brighton. Here, while conducting a fruitful ministry, he continued to develop as a poet. In the Brighton Poetry Circle he encountered the Vedantist Peter Dunn, initiating a close friendship which lasted until Peter's death, not long before Fred's own passing. Much of their extensive correspondence is preserved. Peter was another of the ten friends described in Fred's cycle of 1991.

Some friendships are chequered,
    some safe as a calm sea.
Why am I so relaxed
    in your company?

I see you in my mind's eye,
    tall, frailer now, and spare,
looking a trifle bewildered,
    but likely to get there.

A naturalist by nature,
    you might be Gilbert White
describing a black-cap
    in the letters you write

to me, letters that express
    a poet's sensitivity
to the world around us, too rare
    for recycling. We

first met, two would-be poets,
    eager to learn our craft;
unsure if Dylan Thomas
    was inspired or daft:

not two, but a little group,
    unknown and likely to be;
very chuffed to be published
    in the same anthology.

Your hero was Edward Thomas,
    gloomy in the Weald of Kent;
mine Frost, the sophisticated
    American innocent.

I keep *Death of a Scarecrow*
    always close at hand.
Watching the Muck Fleet: for Owen
    waves its magic wand

over me each time I read it;
    and *The Children Away*
sends a shiver down my spine
    however bright the day.

* * * * *

When circumstances scattered us
    you found a new role
caring for disturbed children
    in a special school.

What was it motivated you
    to give up your best years
to understanding a child's
    fury and fears?

Was it the bitter memory
    of your deprived childhood?
That basement existence
    you would forget if you could?

Or your sense of oneness
    with all created things:
your generosity and compassion
    towards underlings?

It strengthens our friendship
    that our minds are open;
I respect your attraction
    to Vedanta and Zen;

for to me, being a Christian
    in no way forbids
enjoyment of the Gita
    and the Upanishads.

(As for Zen, it's fun turning
    truth upside-down!
and fashionable to make Jesus
    into some sort of clown!)

* * * * *

What walks we had in the days
    when my legs and your heart
were stronger! Every step
    was a fresh start

into the world of nature;
    but how difficult for us
to get you out of the Reserve
    in time for the bus!

Don't tell me it's untrue;
    'We travelled in my Renault' –
One mustn't confuse Reality
    with what we think we know!

Fred Pratt Green: *Ten Friends: P.E.D.*

THE UPANISHADS

His one stout sycamore leg
Breaks to a brilliant orange rash;
His touchwood cross, encased with bark,
Veers to a breeze of Spring – how brash
Those niggling winds that find their mark
Where gales had failed to topple him –
And snaps off short. Fortuitous trash
Returns to mould.
Skylarks are silent, owls begin to shout,
And, as they ease their lilac bodies out
The glistening worms grow bold
To draw his rotten jacket under:
This fallen god is anybody's plunder.
Jackdaws shall pick his woollen brains
To warm their squabs, mice nest
In guts of straw, the farmer's golden grains
Transfix with green his everlasting rest,
Till Death, in turn, topple their tawny sway.
At stubble-time,
Haloed with speedwell, slimed across, and grey,
Stares from the ground a papier mâché grin
Defying Winter's ineluctable rime
To do him in.

Peter Dunn: *Death of a Scarecrow*

Under grey skies I sit here
on a grassed-over lay-by,
making uncomfortable use of
an unseasonable deck-chair.
Gazing plaintively at hills
too depressed to throw off
their burden of cloud, aware
of near-by cows flicking off
imaginary flies, thereby proving
we are all slaves to habit,
I sit here, chilled to the marrow;
and will do so tomorrow.

Nevertheless, my dear Peter,
I have recently feasted
at Little Salkeld Mill on
Luaka tea, and scones
of stone-ground flour,
served by a flaxen-haired
maiden of irreproachable
Viking ancestry, lulled
by the stunning sound
of real water, turning
an aboriginal wheel. But
isn't this thirst for tea
at four o'clock precisely
just another English habit,
like cursing the weather?

Being a Vedantist, agree
that all kinds of weather
are equally expressions
of the One, as is habit
and breaking habit. So,
as I break my habit
of not writing to you,
I am somewhat disappointed
not to be gaining merit.
But it troubles me more
that the stone-ground flour
has no merit either.
Or have I misunderstood
the doctrine? If so, Peter,
put it down to sitting here
in a grassed-over lay-by
cursing the English weather.

Fred Pratt Green: *Letter from a Lay-By* (1980)

Peter and Ruby Dunn (facing camera)
at Fred's eightieth birthday lunch

On radio, once, I heard a Hindu sing
a hymn to Krishna in an alien tongue,
played on a sitar, unlike anything
I was used to; nearer to something sung,
perhaps, in Taizé. Then I grew aware
not of the unfamiliar and suspect,
but of an adoration I could share,
and had no need, for Christ's sake, to reject.
I understood how ancient was my past;
that Hindu Vedas and the Jewish Psalms
declare a common origin, outlast
wars of religion and today's alarms.
Why Christ *or* Krishna? I was in no mood
for confrontation in the name of God.

Fred Pratt Green: *Sonnet for Peter Dunn*

SYDNEY TREMAYNE

Although the beginning of Fred's friendship with Sydney Tremayne cannot be dated with any certainty, it is likely their first encounter occurred not long after that with Fallon Webb, who was himself a friend of Sydney Tremayne. Though born in Ayr, hometown of Robert Burns, it was for the poetry of John Milton that he had greater regard. At the age of 17, he got a job on a newspaper under the delusion it would help in his ambition to become a writer. He continued to work as a journalist, and by 1951 was a leader-writer on a national paper. Besides his poetry, he published some novels.

Sydney was celebrated as another of Fred's ten friends in his 1991 sequence.

I am reading your poems tonight in bed,
trying to reconcile your two selves:
the leader-writer for the popular press,
an exile in the metropolis you hated
and longed to escape; and the Scots poet,
sparing of emotion, in love with words,
too precise, perhaps, for present taste,
but master of images that exactly fit
a memory, telling us how you overcame
greyness and deadness at the sight of swans
'scudding for Berwick under a dark sky.'

What drove you to London? Was it ambition?
Was Glasgow too provincial? the money less?
I meant to ask you but lacked the courage.
You struck me as conservative, reflective,
not the type to be Rothermere's stooge,
or Beaverbrook's. Ah, this is interesting!
Each of us has a poem on Night-Driving:
mine has a brilliantly-contrived ending,
which is deprecated by the best critics;
yours is cool, closely-observed, ironic.
How well you capture nature's changing moods.

You were reticent about your poetry,
never anxious to read it to your friends,
as Tennyson was, and some lesser lights.
Nevertheless Chatto and Windus seemed,
poetically, a good address, and critics,
if they took any notice, were approving;
but your slender volumes made no splash
and were not reprinted. Believe me,
I thought you a better poet of the period,
though smaller in stature, than Edwin Muir,
and tonight I am confirming that opinion.

A memory stabs me. You and Constance
had come to dinner. It was a long evening,
full of talk, of politics, of poetry.
At midnight I mentioned hot-water bottles,
at one in the chilly morning I yawned
cavernously, and you glanced at the clock;
at two you gathered up Constance, and went,
to begin work. A letter from Constance
falls out of your book. She still grieves
for you in that house under the Torridon
Mountains, in the wilds of Wester Ross,
where you escaped at last from servitude.

Fred Pratt Green: *Ten Friends: S.T.*

This city, spouting like a school of whales,
Swims in the morning mist, no thing of walls
But massive and alive, malignant, sooty.
Come spring, come holiday, come sun's harpoon,
Leap from a cloud to pierce this hide of stone,
Free Jonah from the belly of the city.
If joy escapes, the world will have no pity.
If joy dives down, shadows will balk the sun.
Shoot straight, my song, and let the daylight in,
And Jonah cast his waistcoat on the jetty.

Sydney Tremayne: *Holiday*

MARK BOURNE

Fred was comfortable with friends who did not share his religious views, especially so when they were creative. The friendship with Mark, another poet but a convinced atheist, was unusual in that the pair met very occasionally in forty years. Mark recalls that the only lasting meeting was when Pratto (as he knew him) made a short stop with the Bournes in Machynlleth. 'He, generous as ever, stood us lunch in Chester; and I recall a walk round here, in the lovely Llynfant valley, when he pointed out some corn wheat, which I've been able to identify ever since… He was both warm and clever: his description of my views being those of 'a believing atheist' has never been bettered.'

What comes of poetry competitions
is rarely poetry of excellence.
Your poem was a comfortable winner
despite echoes of Dylan Thomas.
You wrote, thanking me.
This was the beginning of our friendship.

Is it so easy to give up poetry?
Only necessity, surely, made you stick
to breeding pigs and chicks.
When they proved a bad investment,
you migrated to Machynlleth,
in alien Wales.

There, on the slopes of Cader Idris,
you finally settled,
hopefully carving a caravan park
out of that unaccommodating terrain.
Tired of difficult tourists,
you sold the site.

It was then you discovered a gift
for soft porn and modelling
(in beautiful cement, of course!).
Soon, to our admiration and envy
articles bearing your name appeared
in prestigious papers.

We loved your broadcast stories
about Italy.
They dug deep into human nature, kinder
than we expected. Temperamentally,
Italy suits you better than Wales.
How strange, then,

It was on the side of a Welsh mountain
you started to recreate,
in miniature, the architectural wonders
of the Italian Renaissance. Now tourists
return in droves to photograph them.
The world's press is taking notice.
You, who were always a personality,
are now a celebrity.

All this time we corresponded.
When I was slow to reply,
you relied upon a mutual friend
(bird-watching in Brighton) for news.
In forty years we have met once.
Thanks to you, our friendship
is still firm.

In one of my wilder flights
of imagination,
I visualise you
as a Cader Idris sort of person:
not uncongenial when in a good mood;
but formidable when confronted
by fools or brash neighbours.

The mountain image intrigues me.
Like Cader Idris,
you are a maverick, a one-off.
I see you, a lonely figure,
climbing towards a snow-clad peak,
armed with an ice-pick.

Fred Pratt Green: *Ten Friends: M.B.*

Mark Bourne

47

CRAIG YR ADERYN

For Iola, gaoled for the Welsh language

I climbed up the hill at morning,
up the rungs of light,
and pulled the sun down to my eyes,
to my height.

And things flew out like motes, dark, free;
a raven clearing the cliff,
a pipit spinning aside, a cormorant's arrow,
fast and stiff.

And all that breathed was free, and flew,
a broken wheel round the sun,
and turned in circles of its own,
like life begun.

And that was the day you went to gaol,
when everything but man
swept round the rock at its will, on strings
of the sun.

There on the hill of exploding birds
I pondered the Celt who
tossed the world away for words, and spurned
sun like you.

I buried my head in the sands of light,
in the too bright day,
but nothing could extinguish them, the birds
you threw away.

Mark Bourne: *Craig yr Aderyn*

As Fred and Marjorie moved to Brighton a new national financial crisis introduced a further period of austerity. Funds to pay for imports were restricted, and food rationing was more severe than anything experienced during the war. By October 1947, the bacon ration had been reduced to one ounce a week. On the world stage, on 15 August 1947 British rule ended in India after 163 years.

Within a year, the National Health Service was born, perhaps the most sweeping of the post-war reforms. It included 2,751 hospitals offering free hospital care and thousands of general practitioners offering free consultation.

The Universal Declaration on Human Rights was also proclaimed in 1948. Thirty years later, the anniversary was marked by a service in Westminster Abbey, for which Fred wrote *Incantation on Human Rights*.

INCANTATION ON HUMAN RIGHTS

Celebrate the Declaration on Human Rights:
may it never be a substitute for action!

I

Celebrate the struggle for human rights
the oldest struggle in history
except the struggle to survive –
and survival, also, is a human right:

the struggle against oppressive rulers
of Church and State;
the struggle against racist regimes,
against grasping landlords,
against greedy employers,
and greedy workers;
the struggle against a soulless bureaucracy,
against earth's polluters,
against sex discrimination,
the struggle against *(specific to occasion)*,
the struggle for *(specific to occasion)*,
the fight to end poverty,
the fight to end injustice,
the fight to help the afflicted,
the fight of humanity…

II

Do not forget Robert and William Kett
and the honest citizens of two shires
who met, unarmed, on Mousehold Heath
to present their reasonable demands
to an already frightened Establishment.
It ended, of course, in bloody death:
it was a long time ago…

God, tell us
how to get justice without violence
and when we have got it
how to prevent it become injustice.

III

I was fed by hands of charity,
they were kind hands,
but it isn't charity I want
though I'm starving,
said the nameless refugee.

I was grateful for your gesture of goodwill,
it was a sincere gesture,
but it isn't a gesture I want,
when I'm refused the job,
said the coloured immigrant.

I looked into your eyes of pity,
they were troubled eyes,
but it isn't pity I want,
when they torture me,
said the political dissident.

What we want is justice, they cry,
a fair share for all, that is justice,
a fair chance for all, that is justice,
a fair trial for all, that is justice.

How can we help them to get justice?

IV

Name them and do not forget them,
the dissidents of the Left and Right.
Remember Orlov, Scharansky, Ginzburg.
Remember William Beausire, last seen
in 1975 in a Chilean centre
for the badly-tortured;
do not forget them

V

They say they may even believe
they are exercising *their* rights
when they kick us about;
they are exercising *their* rights
when they shut us out
of their privileged lives;
they are exercising *their* rights
when they beat us up
in their prison cells;
they are exercising *their* rights
when they shoot us down
in the angry streets.

VI

When the time comes, soon or late,
shall *we* be within our rights
if we kick *them* about,
if we shut *them* out,
if we beat *them* up,
if we shoot *them* down?
God, tell us
how to break the vicious circle
of injustice and revenge;
how when freedom is won
to prevent it from becoming a new form of bondage.

Celebrate the Declaration on Human Rights:
may it never be an excuse for inaction.

Fred Pratt Green: *Incantation on Human Rights*

CHARLES BANKS REMEMBERS THE DOME

At the time of Fred's death, Charles Banks was a fellow supernumerary minister in the Norwich Circuit. He was superintendent of the Dome Mission from 1981–1986.

Preaching in the Brighton Dome was never an easy experience. The building is part of the Royal Pavilion complex built in 1817 for the Prince Regent (later George IV) and the Dome itself was the exercise arena for his horses. The city authorities developed it into a concert hall so that by 1934 it seated 2200 people. The hall lacked the atmosphere and intimacy of even the largest church and if it had been used for some secular pursuit on the Saturday night it was not altogether ready for worship the next day. Everything suggestive of Christian worship had to be imported, the cross, the flowers, the hymn-sheets, the lectern. The organ console had to be raised from beneath the stage. All this had to be done after 5pm on the Sunday. The preacher was called upon to throw his voice and personality across the arena's vast expanse and in the days of the Revd Fred Pratt Green there was no microphone to help him. Mr Green's preaching was described as *'incisive and lucid with touches of winsome humour and quiet persuasiveness'*. He gave the impression of a man of *'great sincerity with a cultured mind'*. He confessed to me that he did not feel it to be quite his scene. When later microphones became available the large congregations of the fifties and sixties had declined and with them some of the inspiration.

Pastoral care of the congregation was also not easy. At first, the Dome congregation, as distinct from the Dorset Gardens church congregation which maintained it, had its own week-day activities. On a Sunday, the stewards would sit strategically in the hall to look after people in their sections. This fell away as the congregation became a small core of church supporters and a large penumbra of visitors. A register of casual attenders was impossible to maintain. Eventually the popularity of Sunday evening TV, the cost of travel to the town centre, the changing role of Brighton as a day-trip resort instead of a longer-stay holiday venue, and the almost nation-wide switch to morning worship contributed to the decline in Dome worship. When the town authorities required the use of the Dome on a Sunday, often at short notice and for a more lucrative booking, the break in the continuity of worship made the work difficult.

Dorset Gardens Brighton

Every minister enjoyed times of inspiration. One such was the Christmas Carol service when all 2200 seats would be filled. These high experiences became fewer in spite of the efforts made by preachers and church members. The idea of using the Dome for worship was launched by Aldom French in 1907 and was a fine one in its day. It became an idea which had run its course and in 1994 the service closed.

Charles Banks

FRED AT THE DOME AND DORSET GARDENS

On Sunday, 7 November 1948, Fred, hearing a visitor from Holland was expected to be in his congregation, invited Dhr J. Slavekoorde to read the lesson, it being Remembrance Sunday. He wrote to me in December 2000, recalling the occasion:

I had never done such a Reading before as a young chap, so it was quite an experience. But I did and it was a great success, just standing before an audience of over 2,000. The last words I did in Dutch and English. Mr Pratt Green was thrilled with my Reading.

The taking of this opportunity to add an international aspect to the occasion was a typical touch for Fred and especially appropriate so soon after the Second World War and the occupation of the Netherlands by Germany. Dhr J. Slavekoorde contributed two articles to later Dome Mission newsletters concerning the very different form of worship to which Dutch Calvinists were accustomed. He also sent me copies of these newsletters and Fred's 38th anniversary report of the Dome Mission. This extract reveals some of the challenges faced by Fred.

What an inspiration the Dome Service is! Unique in Brighton, it is doubtful whether there is anything like it anywhere in the country. Its appeal is super-denominational. A Methodist venture, born of the crusading traditions of Methodism, it attracts people of different Christian traditions and many who have no vital contact with the Church but for the service. Those who welcome people as they come in, hearing many a sad story and many a grateful word, know what an influence it exerts in countless lives. And how far some people come!... let this be said: our aim is not merely to hold and increase this great congregation. We might do this (though it is doubtful) by the kind of popular appeal which sacrifices spiritual truth and cheapens worship. Our people do not come because they want entertaining. They come because they want a religion they can understand and that helps them in their daily lives... The Dome Service is at the heart of our work – and it is sound.

246 Ditchling Road

In February 1948, Fred's sermons were on God's remedy for (1) fear (2) worry (3) depression and (4) boredom. During his first months, Fred reviewed the whole range of activity at the Dorset Gardens headquarters, including important social work on the premises by outside organisations. Much was thriving, such as the uniformed organisations, women's meetings, the guild and social club. He looked too at sections of society they were not serving well, including the need for a mixed youth club for those aged 15–24, hopefully reaching out also to the non-churchgoers in the neighbourhood. He was concerned that the class-meeting, or its modern equivalent, had so small a place in church life.

It can be revealed that Marjorie shopped for meat at Chapman (Butchers) Ltd, at Number 11 Saint James Street, which adjoined Dorset Gardens. The family's needs for eggs, fats, cheese, bacon and sugar were met by Osbornes Stores Limited at Number 8. How do I know? The ration books were preserved among Fred's papers. In the latter part of their stay, the manse was at 246 Ditchling Road, photographed left.

MEMORIES OF TWO YOUNG DOME WORSHIPPERS

I well remember how much it was frowned upon when members deserted their own congregations to attend the Dome Mission in Brighton, on a Sunday night, in order to hear the Rev. Fred Pratt Green lead worship and preach. As a young teenager in the early nineteen-fifties, my parents took me with them to the Dome most Sundays and I was awe-inspired to be part of a congregation of some 2,000 worshippers. It was this dynamic atmosphere which gave me my first vision of the vast extent of the People of God, compared with the confines of one's own particular church building and fellowship.

I recall how on one occasion the subject of the sermon was 'Reconciliation', the meaning of which at 13 I didn't understand. So I decided to start counting the number of times he used the expression and when it got up to twenty, I gave up. But as I grew older, I never heard the word 'reconciliation' without thinking of the Rev. Fred Pratt Green, and of that particular visit to the Dome.

Nowadays as a Local Preacher, I feel very privileged to use so many of Fred's hymns in my services and am thrilled when so many people say to me afterwards how much the hymns have meant to them. In my opinion there is no doubt that Fred Pratt Green was the greatest hymn writer of our day and a worthy Methodist successor to Charles Wesley.

As I look back in my own Christian pilgrimage, I am certain that the influence I received as a teenager from my Sundays at the Dome has helped to fashion my life today and to equip me both as Local Preacher and a Circuit Steward.

Yvonne M. Whitehead

The seats were squeaky; though comfortable. In those days there was a large choir of which I was a member presided over by a wonderful organist, Basil Weymark, who has since died. The pre-service organ music was always appreciated but it was after the service that Basil would treat us to some marvellous things, Finlandia and the Bach Toccata and Fugue to name but two. In those days the Dome Mission always had a Wesley Deaconess to assist in the work and in Mr Green's time she was Sister Mary Randall who on retirement shared the Greens' home in Norwich.

The congregational singing was wonderful. I always say I fell in love with the Methodist Hymn Book before I came really to know the Lord. After Ancient & Modern (I attended Church of England Sunday School) I found the contents of the hymnbook very refreshing.

There were about 40 stewards in those days who, after taking up the collection, processed though the Hall (longest serving first, tailing back to the newer people) they would then turn to face the platform and choir while the offertory prayer was said.

While in Brighton, Mr Green started a Tuesday Fellowship in the Dorset Gardens Church, services which were themed and very popular. I remember one series containing addresses on Saint Francis and Confucius amongst others and how amusing Mr Green could be when talking to us.

Maureen J. Knell

Maureen Knell, in her letter to me, also recalled memorable lines from poems written in Fred's Brighton days between the South Downs and the sea. Some were from his poem *December Dawn*. Others were from a long poem *One Minor Poet to Another*, addressed to Fallon Webb.

Lying awake in the well of darkness
I heard three sounds:
the despairing, half-strangulated
cry of a sea-bird,
the sea pacing the floor of the world,
and your breath in sleep.

Was it the gull's wandering ghost
crying to my ghost
halted me at the panic precipice
where, duped by sleep,
I woke, thinking the sweat on my face
was the sting of the sea?

Your breath in sleep, coming and going
like a trustful child,
dissolved the nightmare world in me
and my ghost cried:
O my love, could we but hear His Breath
who never sleeps!

Not once you stirred, until the rose
of a December dawn
flowered for you in the garden of France,
and as you caught your breath
I heard sleep slip from your body
with how deep a sigh.

Fred Pratt Green: *December Dawn*

Our verse, I said in idle talk,
is different as chalk from cheese
(was mine the cheese and yours the chalk?);

since when I have been ill at ease,
confounded by comparisons
not calculated much to please!

Now as I stand on our South Downs,
more beautiful for lack of trees,
and curse the crude, encroaching towns –

I stand on chalk and nibble cheese!

Fred Pratt Green: Extract from *One Minor Poet to Another*

In 1985, Fred was invited to write a hymn for the 100th anniversary of the building of the Dorset Gardens church. A Methodist church had been on the site since 1808. The words appear in Appendix 2 of this book. A tune for the occasion was written by Malcolm Davey, the organist of the Central United Reformed Church whose choir and congregation were sharing worship with the Dorset Gardens congregation. No relatives of the late Mr Davey have been found, but a copy of the tune can be obtained from Stainer & Bell Ltd.

Now the Dorset Gardens premises are being rebuilt to serve a new century as they fulfil Fred's words *The Church of Christ in every age, beset by change but Spirit led, must claim and test its heritage and keep on rising from the dead.*

The end of Fred's Brighton years were marked by the publication by the Hand and Flower Press of his first poetry collection *This Unlikely Earth*, dedicated to T. W. & G. R. Ramsey. The poem *That World and This* is one of the 27 poems.

Before the Dreamer tossed a casual spark
on tinder of flesh-to-be and lit the fire
that burns us, is beacon to us in the dark,
the world, my loved, was ignorant of desire.
Tethered to the skirts of the sun, it kept
within the Dream its unpretentious course:
nothing lusted or loved in it, nothing slept,
nothing cried out in rapture or remorse;

only the crack of ice-packs shook the air,
thunder in the mountains, tumultuous rain
pelting a waste of sea through millennia
barren of meaning, innocent of pain,
of the lion's rage, the lover's kiss.
Or did He know that world would father this?

Fred Pratt Green: *That World and This*

SHIRLEY'S GENTLE HILLS

Fred and Marjorie moved in 1953 to Shirley's gentle hills, adjoining the Green Belt to the south of London.

Fred came to Shirley when I was twelve. He is the first Methodist minister I can really remember as a person. In Sunday School his prowess as a hymn writer was emphasised to us when we received the new Sunday School Hymn Books at about the same time as he arrived. It contained a hymn by 'Our Minister' which made us feel really 'on the map'. We learned it for his first Sunday School Anniversary with us and he was most touched by our rendition. The hymn was *Let my vision Lord, be keen and clear this day*, and this has remained with me since. I <u>still</u> sing it when I am climbing hills! Fred was very good with the young people at Shirley and we in turn adored him. I was told of his account of this hymn to our Shirley youth group, that it referred to climbing a hill near Leeds when he was a theological student. He took a girlfriend up 'the difficult route' and they got lost in the fog! I later studied in Leeds and felt convinced that the hill was either Otley Chevin or Ilkley Moor – but I do not know for sure. The girlfriend was never identified as Mrs Pratt Green. [It was most likely that the friend was an actress: his parents did not feel this was the right kind of liaison for a Methodist theological student!] I remember Fred wrote a hymn for our boys' choir in about 1954, which they sang at Easter. [As Heather Dean records it was sung to the tune of 'This joyful Eastertide'; it may have been an early version of this text.] Fred was thus entrenched in our young minds at Shirley as a poet and hymnwriter way back in the 1950s. I also remember him presiding at a <u>very</u> simple Holy Communion Service one night – something of an unusual event at the time.

Heather Dean neé Wheelhouse

The subsidence at the front entrance to the church became dangerous and something had to be done quickly. £2,000 was needed AT ONCE. So Fred set up a Gift Day almost on the spur of the moment, I think it was raised in the matter of hours. This is a tiny amount compared to that raised in recent years, but in those days a great achievement. All down to Fred's enthusiasm, he was that sort of man.

Eileen Goodwin

Fred called the 12-foot long pulpit 'The Captain's Bridge'. Dave Jackman, who attended Shirley in his youth, gave these quotables to work-colleague Alan Barber:

♦ When Fred was speaking from 'The Bridge', he made it seem as if he was speaking directly to you.
♦ When somebody else was speaking or singing he always managed to look interested.
♦ He liked Fred because he wasn't T.T. and whisky and Guinness were his favourite tipples.
♦ Fred got him interested in poetry, including that of Betjeman and Auden, the latter's *Night Mail* especially.

I'll start by admitting I'm biased; I had a very high regard for Fred, which started during his ministry at Shirley and has continued ever since. He was a warm, friendly person, who always seemed to be smiling. He appealed to all ages; a fine writer, skilled speaker and great preacher. The Foreword to the Silver Jubilee brochure displays Fred's typical writing style.

Alan Barber

Shirley Methodist Church is situated in the heart of suburbia, that phenomenon the superior have satirised (and, as often as not, chosen to live in!), that monstrosity or demi-paradise, or something between according to our view of it. We are a typical suburban congregation, with a predominance of the young and middle-aged, and we are a family church, remarkably so even for suburbia. We are suburban in outlook, behaviour and ability. We do not lack potential leaders, for many of us are 'executives' in other walks of life. We are free, also, from those disturbing social cleavages which, though fast vanishing, afflict churches in certain areas. Our car park may be full on Sundays, and on occasion it may be difficult to find a parking place without obstructing someone's right of way, but no section of the church community, though car-less feels inferior. Human nature everywhere is apt to be awkward, and even the redeemed are not without faults; but we may claim to be a singularly happy and harmonious, as well as homogenous, church.

continued on next page

SUBURBIA

No doubt we exhibit some of the defects of suburbia. We may be too much *at ease in Zion*, too complacent, too ready to make the success of our church an excuse for not exerting ourselves overmuch. We may be disinclined, some of us, after a double dose of the London rush-hour to leave our homes in order to share in Christian fellowship or to support a worthy cause by our personal presence.

However anxious we are to combat the reputed coldness of suburbia, it is not easy for us to get to know each other on Sundays. Our church lobby is so small we may have to be content with a passing word or nod. We are baffled by the simple problem of finding out which are the numerous 'strangers' and making them feel at home.

Shirley Methodist Church seeks to serve a neighbourhood in which the Church of England is the only other Christian community fully at work. We must apply our Methodism in the sphere of church government, and those who would enter into the official life of our church must become Methodists, but we hold out the right hand of fellowship to all who accept the lordship of Christ, rejoice to have them with us at worship, and invite them to the Lord's Table. We also look forward to a closer fellowship with our Anglican friends, if high policy and local desire make this possible.

Fred Pratt Green: Part of Foreword to Shirley Methodist Church Silver Jubilee Booklet

The Church membership in March 1956 was 406. There were 45 names on the Cradle Roll and Sunday School membership was 281. There were 60 Guides, 40 Brownies, 62 Scouts, a Cub Pack, a Fellowship of Youth with 70 members, a Ladies' Sewing Guild numbering 50, a Young Wives' & Mothers' Circle attracting a membership of 90, and a 28-strong choir. Fred began a well attended Church Fellowship with weekly talks on topical subjects viewed from a Christian standpoint.

For the Church's Golden Jubilee Concert in 1981, which was preceded by light music from the early thirties, Fred wrote a Dramatic Prologue, setting the background scene in 1931 in terms of the divided Methodist Church and the national and international situation. Eileen Goodwin and Alan Barber's son, Andrew, formed half the cast. Oboist Maurice Checker performed at this concert (see page 18). Fred also wrote a hymn for the occasion, which he later adapted for more general use.

How right that we should offer
to God unceasing praise,
yet mark the Church's seasons,
her high and holy days:
then share with us this story
we would not leave untold –
our fifty years of learning
to be Christ's flock and fold.

In times of growing tension,
of stubborn social ills,
as London spread still closer
to Shirley's gentle hills:
God's servants built a Church here
to meet a people's needs,
whose names we justly honour,
their foresight and their deeds.

What fifty years accomplished
we frankly would recite,
alike success and failure
set down in black and white.
Yet this is hidden from us;
and none but God can trace
how much is our achievement,
how much a work of grace.

Before us lies the future,
with claims we must obey;
we pray we may not face it
our faith in disarray.
Lord God, revealed in Jesus,
your Church, and us, endow
with wisdom, love and courage
to serve your Kingdom now.

Fred Pratt Green: *A Hymn in Celebration of the Golden Jubilee of Shirley Methodist Church*

Serious subsidence led to the Church building being demolished in 1997. This hymn was sung again in 2001 in a new church where there was no longer a bridge for the Captain but still a thriving society facing the challenges of a new century.

In 1957, Fred was appointed as the first separated chairman of the newly created York and Hull Methodist District. It amused him to find that when the previously separate districts found it difficult to find unanimity as to whom they wished to commend to the Methodist Conference as chairman, a Lancastrian was sent to sort it out. When in 1964 he retired from the chairmanship to go back into Circuit for his last active ministry, he was presented with the Folio Society's reprint of *The Natural History of Selborne*, by the eighteenth-century naturalist Gilbert White, who was also an Anglican priest. It included the inscription 'He came – a Stranger. He leaves – beloved'. It remained with his books until his death, alongside a copy of The Revd Keble Martin's *The Concise British Flora in Colour*. Several members of Synod have commented on his skill in conducting meetings, his efficiency in transacting the necessary business, and his gift of leavening tense discussions with his ever-present sense of humour.

During his chairmanship, Fred wrote his most ambitious long poem, in which he tackled ecclesiastical and theological problems. It was motivated by a very real concern for a friend, Ralph Lawrence, and its prosody was no accident. He deliberately attempted a fairly loose structure, with long rhythms, because he wanted to invite a meditative approach to the text.

Fred considered it probable that the work was more a statement of free churchmanship than a poem. On several occasions he considered rewriting it; but each time felt he could not improve on the original.

I

Here in our northern city, as snow falls on a minster so old
It never escapes now disfigurement of ladder and scaffold,
I offer a Dissenter's thanks for servants of the Word made flesh,
And for yourself, already revered and reverend, and wish
That York were Canterbury and I at your priesting, to raise
My hand in schismatic blessing, my voice in unity of praise.

II

Today you kneel, in a cathedral rich in prelatic ghosts,
With the young men who give all, not knowing what all costs,
You, Christ's pensioner, whose only gift is the precious little
That's left; not life's ashes at bedtime, but a gay committal
To Christ of a lifetime's harvest and a harvester's rest.
The youngest never gave himself with so infectious a zest.

III

Thinking to follow, from afar, the vows a priest makes, I turn
In my boyhood's prayer-book to the Ordinal, there to burn
My fingers on the dull ashes of a past that has kept its heat
These fifty years. I hear again the bells of Childwall calling
Across cornfields when my life lay fallow, waiting for the falling
Seed of the Gospel, a high bell scolding my Sabbath-sullen feet.

IV

How majestic the Te Deum! How tedious the Litany! How old,
Older than God, the Rector! How warm a hand in mine! How cold
The crumbling sandstone effigies! Say it was a false start
Or firm foundation; that chance, or providence, drew me apart
Into another sheep-fold, where, wanting to give all,
I stumble towards an ordination sans bishop and sans cathedral.

V

Rashly I ask: down episcopal fingers travels what grace
And authority? Is this magic? or the Unfailing Source
Channelling Himself to us through swamp and desert? Or nothing worse,
Or better, than the dressing-up in cope and mitre of a commonplace
Process? Or is it true, as the Dissenter in me contends,
That each of us is a priest on whom God has laid His hands?

VI

Consider Cranmer; how, trapped between Tudor patronage
And the Bloody Tower, he framed these liturgies for an age
When words were the deadly swords men fenced with. Without the least
Doubt he ordains you, in this rite, both minister and priest –
A Genevan minister, a Roman priest, which of us knows?
So well he cultivated his hybrid Anglican rose!

VII

It troubles me that at worship's centre, at Altar and Table,
The priesthood separates us, speaks only discomfortable
Words, forbidding me to kneel with you before Christ the Host,
Except by a circumvention. If I were to invite you
Would you kneel at my side? Should we be able to break through
These impregnable positions, if we loved to the uttermost?

VIII

Small wonder He warned the Twelve a divided house would fall;
But they, like us, were too busy disputing their apostolical
Pretensions to listen. What conflicts, waged in His name, besmirch
The unrepented centuries! How near to falling is His House!
Is the sin yours or mine? Or are we all without excuse?
Christ, by Your Body broken, unite us, Your broken Church!

IX

A truce, then, to controversy. It is prayer spans the abyss
Of our separation, is the deep therapy that must cure this
Sickness of Christ's Body. Freed from entanglement of words.
I pray for all who dispense Word and Sacrament in the Lord's
Church; for all who seek out His sheep that are dispersed abroad;
For all who, not following with us, serve compassion's Lord.

X

Hearing you sing *Veni, Creator Spiritus*, I confess
That all is mystery. The Spirit, blowing where He lists,
Fans the weak flame of our faith into a consuming fire
Of devotion, moves mountains of doubt, is tireless when we tire,
Sets us apart for His use, with an iron tenderness
Shapes our vocation like a potter the clay resists.

XI

To be set apart is our benefit and disability. To some
We shall be ambassadors of a country alien as Siam;
To some parasites, impostors, figures of fun; to others
Fathers-in-God and confessors, fellow-labourers and brothers-
In-Christ. And what are we? Ordinary men seeking to please
God, whose haloes, hollow as crowns, do not hide our unease.

continued on next page

ONE GOD, THE FATHER, SON, AND HOLY SPIRIT

XII

Ours is no sheltered life. After the Dove's descent, the Devil
Waylays us in a wilderness where images of good and evil
Are blurred. Though we shall never rig a balance-sheet to cheat
An investor, or stand with the workless in a hungry street,
Or sleep in beds of adultery, we shall confuse stones
With bread, showmanship with sincerity, pulpits with thrones.

XIII

Our voices ring out in a square chapel audaciously, or echo
In gothic rafters with a more subtle insistence, as the ego
Exalts itself in preaching. Like Jonah in Nineveh, we enjoy
Our sadistic denunciations, are quick to resent
A God less ready than we are to punish or destroy,
Who patiently waits for a godless city to repent.

XIV

Today, as priest, you receive the key which unlocks the door
Of a confessional that to Christ's rebels, and His unpriested poor,
Is never (I trust) locked. But, Lord, the thing which confounds
Us is to be shown those running sores, those self-inflicted wounds
We hide under gown and cassock; what comforts us is that we too
Who are both shepherd and sheep, offer and have need of You.

XV

Once upon a peaceful time we should have shepherded the flock
Of Christ by the still waters, in the shadow of the Rock,
With the Wolf for adversary. Now, alas, our Holy Land
Lies open to the invader; every outpost must be manned
Along forgotten frontiers. Driven from familiar pastures,
Our divided flock dwindles, miraculously endures.

XVI

Yet surely this is a time to rejoice in, not to bemoan!
Even in York, where masons are renewing, stone by stone,
The great Church of Saint Peter, where gargoyles keep their grimaces,
An unpredictable future boldly and brashly replaces
The past. A new age beckons us from inter-stellar spaces.
And shall not the Eternal God claim this age as His own?

XVII

So wherever you go, my friend, whether into the thick
Of the battle in the ding-dong streets of a city parish,
Or to lovely decaying villages where men also perish,
Or to the plum of a living plucked from a suburban tree,
May the Lord bless you and keep you, and may the angelic
Hosts watch over you, the blessed saints be your company.

XVIII

At last the ceremonious afternoon, the priesting, ends;
And here, city and minster blotted out, I quietly sit
In contemplation of that bond, closer than between friends,
That mystical unity where in every Christian soul
(O make more tangibly effective, more visibly whole!)
Abides in the One God, the Father, Son, and Holy Spirit.

Fred Pratt Green: *Poem for Ralph Lawrence on his Ordination to the Priesthood*

BACK PAIN CURED

During this period Fred met Herbert Dixon of Thirsk, another of the ten friends remembered in the cycle. Herbert, ahead of his time, combined the practice of conventional medicine with that of osteopathy.

The day I heard of your death
I sent a belated wreath,
with the kind of words that fit,
remembering how we had met
and lost touch, more upset
than I care now to admit.

Let me tell you how it began:
as parson and best man
we shared a wedding day;
and liked each other a lot.
We promised to meet – and forgot;
It often happens, they say.

But life repaired the damage,
when late in our middle age
our paths again crossed
in the same town and place,
as if by a special grace.
How many years we had lost!

On the day that we met again
I was doubled up with pain;
while you, in the years we lost
had acquired the exact skill
I needed. As if by a miracle
you became my therapist.

In fact you had two skills:
the official one that fulfils
the known rules, and the other,
the osteopathic skill
intuitive, mysterious still.
In you both worked together.

So patients came, one and all,
to your clinic and hospital,
convinced only you could cure
their ills. It was town-talk
you had got a woman to walk,
after years in a wheel-chair.

My treatment was quite severe,
and took nearly half a year,
in fortnightly visits. In the end
you cured me of what was wrong
with my spine. No longer young,
I had found myself a friend.

* * * * *

Your terrace house was old,
comfortless and cold.
I was shocked and horrified,
till a neighbour chanced to say:
only weeks before the 'day'
your bride-to-be had died.

That was twenty years ago,
since when you had been slow
to keep up with the street:
'Not a proper life at all,
just clinic and hospital,
with little enough to eat.'

This was kindly neighbour's talk,
but true that with all your work,
and the long hours you kept,
if you had a home at all
it was clinic and hospital;
the house was where you slept.

No need then to be misled:
what with chapel, and first aid,
bowls and photography,
your life was as satisfying,
outgoing and self-denying,
as anyone's life can be.

However, you tried to make
things pleasanter for my sake,
with flowers in the living room,
sweets on my bedside table,
even the parlour habitable,
best of all a hearty welcome.

I knew you from way-back
as the Joker in the Pack;
now, as our friendship grew,
you would prove yourself to be
the life and the soul of the party,
though the party was just two.

This time, we did not forget
to meet again. Yes, we met
each spring or summer, to share
long days in your countryside,
then, venturing far and wide,
beyond Galloway and Ayr.

continued on next page

HERBERT DIXON

Our late friendship, so rich
in happiness for each,
would last a dozen years,
until old age destroyed
your wits, and filled the void
with fantasies and fears.

* * * * *

My last visit was grim:
no flowers in the living-room,
no bed made up for a guest;
only a blank stare
at a stranger standing there,
inexplicably distressed.

You were cared for at the last,
by those who knew you best,
regained your cheerfulness,
and lived in a gentle haze
your few remaining days,
a man many of us still miss.

Fred Pratt Green: *Ten Friends: H.D.*

Photograph of Thurne, Norfolk taken by Herbert Dixon,
who was a fine photographer

Picture by Herbert Dixon on the wall of Fred's room at Cromwell House

BACH; EISTEDDFOD; APOSTOLIC SUCCESSION

I remember Fred Pratt Green, when he was chairman of the York and Hull District, coming to address a small women's meeting in Goole. His subject was hymns and he sat informally at the piano playing and talking to us all as we surrounded him. Perhaps he was discussing hymns with unusual rhythms, for I remember he played *Jesu, priceless treasure*, one of my favourites and *Art thou weary, art thou languid*. He remarked humorously on the translation of the first line but it was a fine old hymn repaying study. It is sadly missing from *Hymns and Psalms*, like *I give my heart to thee, O Jesus most desired* which he played to the lovely tune by J. S. Bach. It says much for his capacity to arouse interest that all this has remained in my mind for forty years!

Some time later he was a judge at a Methodist Eisteddfod, of poems written by various age-groups of children, which my daughter entered. He wrote a comment in his own hand, pointing out that one of her lines didn't exactly scan – but then, she was in tune with modern poets who did not set great store by rhyme or regular rhythm. There was the hymn-writer speaking, whose attention to stress and rhyme are so important, and exemplified in his hymns we sing today.

Joyce Petch, who was Head Girl at Hunmanby Hall School in 1944

Fred Pratt Green is remembered with affection as my first District chairman when I began life as a probationer in 1958.

John W. Ansley

Fred recalled that not a few suspected his appointment as the separated Chairman of District, previously a role carried out by a minister in the area, usually a Circuit Superintendent. These folk thought that the move was a dangerous step towards union with the Church of England and acceptance of the Doctrine of Apostolic Succession. His skills as an administrator, a reconciler and Father-in-God were well tested. Fred and Marjorie loved the Yorkshire countryside and its people, and often returned to the area in later life. To travel with Fred through his old District was to journey with a feast of anecdotes at one's side.

A small hotel near York where Fred often took friends.
The Braleys stayed here with the Greens on a holiday in 1983.

Trinity Church Sutton, London, showing the outer door of which Fred wrote in a hymn for their stewardship campaign:

When the Church of Jesus shuts its outer door,
Lest the roar of traffic drown the voice of prayer:
May our prayers, Lord, make us ten times more aware
That the world we banish is our Christian care.

SOME HEADLINES DURING FRED'S SUTTON YEARS

Krushchev deposed (October 1964)
Chinese explode first A-bomb (October 1964)
Labour elected by a whisker (October 1964)
Death of Churchill (January 1965)
America at war in Vietnam (1965)
Gongs for The Beatles (October 1965)
Tragedy at Aberfan (October 1966)

The Six-Day War (June 1967)
Luther King gunned down (April 1968)
Students riot in France (May 1968)
Tanks crush Prague Spring (August 1968)
Vorster bans MCC tour (September 1968)
Nixon presidency begins (January 1969)
Concorde 002 maiden flight (April 1969)

Armstrong steps on the moon (July 1969)

THE BEATLES ERA

Fred received me and my sister into church membership and, of course, I am now very proud to have a book with commemorative words and his own signature in it as a memory of that occasion and of him. I say that because, at the time, none of us knew that his hymn-writing career was about to take off...Those, who like myself who were teenagers in the 60s, however, would wish to remember him as a man who, despite having no children himself, very quickly engaged with the feeling and aspirations of our generation in those memorable years. He gave us readings of his own poetry at our youth group (and it is as a poet rather than a hymn writer that we remember him).

I also vividly recall a sermon he preached one evening in about 1967. He announced that he had just been out and bought a record; it was *Sergeant Pepper's Lonely Hearts Club Band* by that well known group, The Beatles! He then preached a sermon based on and around the words of the song *She's Leaving Home*. This was not done with any affectation or a desire to be popular; he genuinely engaged with the spirit and words of the song which, of course, was to become a classic. In so doing, he maintained the link and closeness to, as I have said, the generation of which I was a member. It was a privilege and a joy to be one of his young congregation during those fascinating years, and many of us from that generation remember him with great affection.

Richard Partridge, recalling Fred's Sutton ministry

If I had been born 40 years later, I might have been a Beatle!

Fred Pratt Green, who was born in Lancashire, following receipt of a 'Beatle's book' in his last years

Fred often told me that he hoped he might be remembered for his poetry more than for his hymns: so it is especially good to record Richard Partridge's memoir. Fred was very glad to be back in Circuit ministry for his last and happiest itinerant appointment. Here Fred found in his congregation many professional people and those prominent in commerce and industry.

Fred enjoyed the challenge of every age, both in the sense of the changing circumstances of the years, and in the ages of those among whom he ministered. This man, who wore L-plates with enthusiasm for all his life, was naturally at home with each younger generation, enjoying their company and their ideas from which he felt himself privileged to learn. At Sutton, too, with so many people of stature among his charges, he felt a great humility in preaching Sunday by Sunday. From them, he sought to learn about their various workaday duties, anxieties, pressures of decision-making and, in so doing, to be relevant, Sunday by Sunday, to many in encouraging their spiritual growth and their role as God's flamebearers in the wider world. And as always, his spiritual growth and understanding of human behaviour were enhanced by such encounters.

Fred recorded that Sutton's curator, as they called their caretaker, proved to be especially helpful and became a valued friend. Fred was, of course, Superintendent of the Circuit as well as having pastoral oversight of Trinity Church. It was during his years at Sutton that his hymn-writing days began in earnest. But for his poetry, of which the collection *The Skating Parson* was published in 1965, he might well not have been appointed to the committee planning *Hymns and Songs*, the supplement to *The Methodist Hymn-Book*. He might not have responded to their challenge, which required 'Methodism's poet' to try his hand at hymns on subjects that members of that group wanted. When the book was published in 1969, Fred was on the verge of retirement with intentions which did not include the writing of much hymnody.

THE RENAISSANCE OF BRITISH HYMNODY

Albert Bayly

Sometimes Fred has been described erroneously as the person who began the renaissance in British hymnody: in denying this, he spoke of the two principal nonconformists whose work was ahead of his own. Albert Bayly was a Congregationalist minister and had his first hymns published in 1950. The little known text published in 1967 *Beneath the glory of the skies* echoes themes of interest to Fred. Albert was born two years earlier and also wrote poetry.

Beneath the glory of the skies,
With awe our voices rise
In praise and adoration.
The circling constellations show
God's majesty to man below,
His greatness in creation.

Let all that lives in sea and air
God's handiwork declare,
His mysteries unfolding;
While man, God's image, crowns the praise,
And tells the wisdom of His ways;
His love all life upholding.

Most clearly shines in Jesus' face
The glory of God's grace;
By Him was all created:
And when creation's day is past,
Then comes the End, when all at last
In Christ is consummated.

Albert Bayly (1901–1984)

Another Congregationalist, Fred Kaan, a native of Holland, had been writing hymns for his worshippers at Pilgrim Church, Plymouth, and a first book of his texts was published in 1968. His most widely used hymn was written in 1965 to mark Human Rights Day on 10 December. *For the healing of the nations* is given here in its definitive version.

For the healing of the nations,
Lord, we pray with one accord,
for a just and equal sharing
of the things that earth affords.
To a life of love in action
help us rise and pledge our word.

Lead us forward into freedom,
from despair your world release,
that, redeemed from war and hatred,
all may come and go in peace.
Show us how through care and goodness
fear will die and hope increase.

All that kills abundant living,
let it from the earth be banned:
pride of status, race or schooling,
dogmas that obscure your plan.
In our common quest for justice
may we hallow life's brief span.

You, Creator-God, have written
your great name on humankind;
for our growing in your likeness
bring the life of Christ to mind;
that by our response and service
earth its destiny may find.

Fred Kaan (born 1929): *A Hymn on Human Rights*

Fred Kaan

MORE ON FRED'S CONTEMPORARIES

Another Congregationalist, Brian Wren, who was ordained in 1965, came to be linked with Fred Kaan and Fred Pratt Green as the chief nonconformist figures of the renaissance in English hymnody. The definitive version of this striking hymn is a fine example of his work.

Come, cradle all the future generations,
and guard their right to live upon this earth,
lest human deeds, by stealth or conflagration,
snuff out all life, and put an end to birth.

Come, contemplate the sadness of extinction:
a wasted earth, with empty sky and sea,
no mourners to lament its desolation,
no voice, no words, no thought, no eyes to see.

We cannot stifle knowledge or invention.
The ways divide, the choice forever clear:
to drift, and be delivered to destruction,
or wake and work, till trust out-matches fear.

The precious seed of life is in our keeping,
yet if we plant it, and fulfil our trust,
tomorrow's sun will rise on joy and weeping,
and shine upon the unjust and the just.

Our calling is to live our human story
of good and bad, achievement, love and loss,
then hand it on to future shame or glory,
lit by our hope, and leavened by the cross.

Come, let us guard the gateway to existence,
that thousands yet may stand where we have stood,
give thanks for life and, praising our persistence,
enjoy this lovely earth, and call it good.

Brian Wren (born 1936)

Brian Wren

Sydney Carter (born 1915)

Fred Pratt Green, writing in his notebook in 1981 about his contemporaries, records:

It is now usual to link three of us as the chief figures in what Erik Routley calls the contemporaneous renaissance in English hymnody – the three being Fred Kaan, Brian Wren and myself. But it is recognised that the 'father' of the movement (if that is what it is) is Albert Bayly, who has been pioneering in this field since the 1940s, perhaps even earlier.

It may well be that other names will emerge or have already done so. Sydney Carter, in his own sphere, as song writer rather than a traditional hymn writer, has had an immense influence on the 'movement'.

extract continued on next page

Richard Jones pioneered with *God of concrete, God of steel*, though he has written little of importance since. And now Timothy Dudley-Smith is being appreciated by editors of major new hymn-books. He has eleven hymns in the draft list for the projected new *Methodist Hymn Book* – more than either Kaan or Wren. One could name others, notably Michael Hewlett, whose rich vein of humour makes him unique as a hymn writer!

Erik Routley, in the autumn number of *The Hymn*, the bulletin of the Hymn Society of America, has summed the four of us up, in a very frank article:

Albert Bayly: a very modest and humble person who has an extraordinary gift for writing a good text and is as well recognised here as in my own country.

Pratt Green, is the only English Methodist hymn writer since Charles Wesley, and has the most extraordinary way of keeping the standard up. He uses his talents economically. The man is a professional, a jewel.

Fred Kaan, with his violent, dissenting, abrasive style, which, when it comes off, is terrifying and rings the bell…(he then mentions two hymns)

Brian Wren, ferocious, and committed, makes us all feel very cheap and vulgar if we're not as interested in the Third World as he is. He has a poetic talent which is perhaps beyond the other two when he really gets going.

I read this estimate of us with interest – and I think it is fair to us all. Albert Bayly is beautifully delineated. Fred Kaan is perhaps a shade underestimated – probably because Erik (and

others) may think he 'dates' somewhat. I agree that Brian Wren has a fine poetic gift – a lyrical charm – one envies…

Myself? A 'professional!' Erik Routley has said this before, comparing me with another 'professional', Canon Briggs, of an earlier generation. Yes, I admit to being a professional, I know what Routley means. He means that I look on hymn writing as a job to be done, am ready to accept commissions, and am critical enough to see the importance of standards! Yes, this is true. But seeing oneself, as someone else who is knowledgable sees us, is a strange experience.

Fred Pratt Green: *Notes of a Hymn Writer*, his unpublished personal memoir written in 1981.

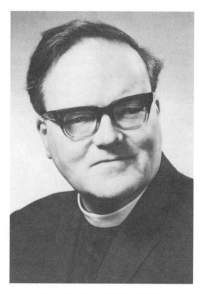

Erik Routley (1917–1982)

As Fred moves into the third age of life it is apposite to quote his perceptive poem *A Teenage World*, defining the beginning of the seventies.

Every evening the elderly used to stroll
Up the High Street to the Town Centre,
Window-shopping. Now it's a teenage world,
Where we walk like aliens without passports,
Hoping to get by. If stared at, we smile
With the defensive bonhomie of the senile.

Out of the corners of our watery eyes
We watch the tight-jeaned youngsters flaunt
Their masculinity in front of girls
Whose cupped breasts arrogantly invite
A doorway petting. Slyly, we think
This was a cup from which we used to drink

When we were young. Milling around, they talk
A foreign language, wear outlandish garb.
A juke box blares. Coffee bars are alive
With a generation beating its time
To cannibalistic rhythms that defeat
Our stiffening joints and spongy feet.

Why are we strangers to our grandchildren?
Why do they contract out of our lives?
The town clock strikes ten. By midnight
We shall all lie between crumpled sheets,
Too far apart to hear each other weep,
One family beneath the low roof of sleep.

STORYTELLING AND HUMOUR

When Jesus wanted to make a point with his disciples he often told a story, and these stories were often dusted with humour. Frequently, too, they referred to near-at-hand objects and familiar life-situations. They must surely have been communicated with a twinkle in the eye, making poker-faced readings of them in church, with solemn voices and not even the glimmer of a twinkle, a distortion of the truth.

In conversation, in his poems, indeed in every part of his ministry, Fred told stories often laced with a mischievous, but never malicious, wit. His ability to observe and remember the fine detail of nature's scenes and of human situations provided a deep well of stories from which he could draw. His gift as a raconteur enlivened any car journey. A touch of humour, graciously delivered, could take a business meeting forward when passions were at breaking point. It could help speed decisions on subjects by which most present were bored.

The picture of Fred as a writer would be incomplete without a selection from his unpublished lighter pieces, many of which carry a serious point alongside their humour.

It's the glossiest kind of high living
that makes an executive tick.
Oh! it's cosy, it's costly, it's crazy,
but a credit-card does the trick.

Our executive houses are roomless;
we have levels and spaces instead.
You should see the Victorian drapings
of our treble-sprung double bed.

We've gone solar for central heating;
it's more energy-saving than gas.
If the temp is inclined to be polar,
we are cross with the sun, not the glass.

Our shavers are closely adjusted
to our sex and our shape and our skin;
and we don't have to queue for the bathroom –
it's hot-tubbing, with everyone in.

Our luxury kitchen is magic:
it conjures up food that's delish.
You have only to touch the right buttons
and – hey presto! – *his* favourite dish.

Twice a week, we consider our figures,
and dine on nutritious nut-chops;
as for bread, it has to be whole-wheat,
stone-ground from the smarter health shops.

When we give a select dinner party
to high-ups we happen to know,
thanks to beautiful hand-cut glasses
our status will never be quo.

Our silk shirts assure our promotion;
our underwear's fashioned to fit.
When we travel, we plan our survival
with a danger-free luxury kit.

With a Bank that is eager to help us,
our future will never be worse.
At the end? Why, the dream of a funeral
in the glossiest jet-propelled hearse!

Fred Pratt Green: *Glossy Living*

This editorial itch to 'alt' a text,
without good reason, backed by common sense,
has gone too far. 'George Herbert will be next,'
I said. He was. Alas! on some pretence
The cream of all my heart was watered down!
The famous dead are easy game. But we,
the living, have a law 'they' can't disown:
our copyright is our security:
they must not 'alt' without permission. So,
the less determined, or less honest, claim:
despite intense research, we do not know
the author's whereabouts, only his name.
To make impossible this nice excuse,
here's my address, sans blessing, sans abuse!

Fred Pratt Green: *Sonnet for Basil Bridge*

Though Fred can't be reached at his new address, his moral right under the 1988 Copyright Act not to have a text amended without permission persists, and vests under his will in Bernard Braley and will vest after his death with another. Requests should be addressed to his publishers Stainer & Bell (address on page ii).

FOR A CHURCH CONCERT

Fred was enthusiastic in writing light pieces for local use. This is typical.

GEORGE and ROSE, a middle-aged couple, are about to go away for the weekend. George is a quiet, pipe-smoking man; Rose is stylish and volatile. There is a short part for WILLIAMS, a taxi driver. ROSE enters, with travelling case, hat-box, etc. She is dressed for a journey. She bustles about, doing last things.

ROSE *(shouting)*: Where are you, George? What are you doing? *(No answer; Rose shows impatience)* We shall be late! GEORGE *enters, also dressed for journey. He is cool and cheerful.*

ROSE: Where on earth have you been?

GEORGE: Obeying orders, my dear.

ROSE: Orders indeed! *(amiably)* Someone has to remember all the things that have to be done, even if we are only going away for the week-end. Have you locked the shed?

GEORGE: Yes, my dear.

ROSE: And left the back-door key with the Masons?

GEORGE: Yes, my dear.

ROSE: And left a note for the milkman cancelling the milk until next Wednesday?

GEORGE: Yes, my dear.

ROSE: Are you sure the gas is turned off?

GEORGE: Yes, my dear.

ROSE: I wish you wouldn't keep on saying 'yes, my dear'.

GEORGE: Now it's my turn, darling. *(Takes out pipe puts it back in his pocket)* Have you packed my red socks?

ROSE: No, I have not! Aunt Mabel would not approve. *(Bustles round)* And you must wear a tie, George. Aunt Mabel is not used to men in casuals. There is nothing casual about Aunt Mabel. *(Restless)* I wish the taxi would come. It must be time.

GEORGE: Williams is never late. *(Moves luggage nearer door)* Is it really necessary to take your hat-box?

ROSE: I must. I want to wear the hat I bought for Joyce's wedding – for church on Sunday morning. You know how much you liked it.

GEORGE: Yes, yes, very fetching. But will Aunt Mabel approve?

ROSE: She will have to, won't she?

GEORGE *(mildly)*: Then, my dear, why shouldn't she put up with my red socks?

ROSE: That's quite different. There's nothing casual about my hat. *(Sits, powders nose)* It must be two years since we had a long week-end together – just us two.

GEORGE *(sotto voce)*: And Aunt Mabel!

ROSE: We must make it another honeymoon – a mini-honeymoon, George dear. Aren't you looking forward to it?

GEORGE *(seriously; showing affection)*: Yes, of course I am.

ROSE: Aunt Mabel is very fond of you. She once said she was thankful I was marrying a man who would look after me.

GEORGE: I do my best.

ROSE *(rising; restless)*: The taxi should be here by now. *(Consults watch)* It's a quarter-past. Williams is usually very reliable.

GEORGE: You did order the taxi?

ROSE *(startled)*: Order the taxi – me? Of course I didn't order the taxi. You always do that.

GEORGE *(calmly: fishing for pipe again)*: Ah, but you said you had to phone Aunt Mabel and would phone for the taxi at the same time – don't you remember? You said 'leave it to me' – don't you remember?

ROSE *(very shaken):* I didn't – did I – Yes, I do seem to remember. *(very upset)* It must have slipped my mind – Oh George, what shall we do? – Phone Williams –

GEORGE: It's too late now. And, besides, Williams is always fully booked on Saturdays.

ROSE: We could go tomorrow.

GEORGE: Sorry, darling. There are no trains to Barton-on-the-Moor on Sundays.

ROSE: What a terrible thing to have happened! Why didn't you remind me? *(very agitated)* Don't stand there, doing nothing. Do something! *(A ring on the door bell)*

GEORGE: I wonder who that can be? *(Rose hurries out. George stands, smiling, pipe in hand. Rose returns, in high spirits)*

IT, A BISHOP AND A SUFFRAGETTE

ROSE: It's the taxi, George. Oh, what a relief! I must have rung Williams up, as I said I would. Isn't it funny how one can forget whether one has done things or not? (WILLIAMS, *the taxi driver, enters to collect luggage*)

ROSE *(to Williams)*: My husband thought I'd forgotten to phone you. We were getting quite agitated. Just these few things, thank you. We're only going away for the week-end. *(Rose goes out. Williams, luggage in hand, turns to George)*

DRIVER: But it was you phoned me sir, not your missus.

GEORGE: That's our secret, Williams, we won't tell her she forgot.

DRIVER: Trust me, sir. I'm a married man myself. *(George goes out, followed by the driver)*

DRIVER *(as he exits)*: Have a nice week-end, sir!

Fred Pratt Green: *Have a nice weekend*

Now God has been desexed
to humour Women's Lib,
because the jade is vexed
at being Adam's rib:
I'll have to grit
my teeth and try
to praise the High
and Mighty IT.

To plead that God is HE
because the Book says so,
has never dealt a she
the faintest body-blow:
I'll have to grit
my teeth and try
to praise the High
and Mighty IT.

With Islam on the rise
the day will come when she
is Ayatolah-ised
By that man Khomeini.
Till then I'll grit
my teeth and try
to praise the High
and Mighty IT.

O God indefinite,
but more defined than X,
I wish I had the wit
t'invent another sex.
Instead I'll grit
my teeth and try
to praise the High
and Mighty IT.

Fred Pratt Green: *A Hymn in Praise of IT*
(May be sung to any decent 6.6.6.6.4.4 4.4. tune)

The other day I had to buy
a Get-Well Card for my Great-Aunt Maud,
who at eighty-three has smashed a knee,
and lies, the terror of Nightingale Ward,
expecting a card from me.

My Get-Well Card cost 50p,
which I don't think too much
for a quite adorable kangaroo
presenting a choice bouquet
to a plump lass in a flowery dress,
stretched out on a golden couch.

Instead of sending it through the post,
with the risk of its being lost,
I took it in person to my Great Aunt Maud,
who lay, the terror of Nightingale Ward,
expecting a card from me.

She took the card from my trembling hand,
her lorgnette from her reticule,
and eyeing it once, and twice, and thrice,
she champed her jaws like a crocodile,
and barked: 'Of great nephews all –
you are the most incredible fool –

'I was in my time,' said my Great Aunt Maud,
'a Pankhurst suffragette.
I married the Movement instead of a lord,
and hit three policemen over the head
(one with concussion and one stone dead) –

and you have the impertinence, Nephew,' she said,
'with your weak chin and your slovenly slouch,
to buy me a card with a silly girl
ensconced on a quite preposterous couch:
and couldn't you see that the kangaroo
has a baby in its pouch?
a baby in its pouch?'

Fred Pratt Green: *The Get-Well Card*

So Durham says there was no Resurrection:
which is surprising, when you think if it!
No wonder prelates plead with him to quit,
suspecting Satan wangled his selection.
All look to Canterbury for direction;
but he, poor Primate, is required to knit
irreconcilables, and needs must sit

upon that fence which is our best protection
against collapse of what we hold most dear.
This being so, we are disposed to cheer
my Lord of Durham, who now makes it clear
that when the Truth, if properly inspected,
by sifting fact from fable, is corrected,
he still believes what he has just rejected.

Fred Pratt Green: *Explanatory Sonnet at a Time of Controversy*

NORWICH

And so to Fred and Marjorie's retirement, in a pleasant semi-detached house with a not-too-large garden, and with time for real possibilities of pastel-painting, roaming the Norfolk countryside, a study of Shakespeare sonnets, time for writing more poetry, as well as acceptance of a fairly light schedule giving a hand when needed in the Norwich Methodist Circuit.

But what a marvellous morning! Norfolk has a poor public image. When we decided to retire here, our friends were far from approving. 'You'll be snowed up all winter;' 'It's off the map, nobody will visit you;' 'It's flat!' they said. All complete nonsense!

NORFOLK, though not mountainous, has variety of landscape, flat to the East, but with the Broads to compensate; it is not off the map nowadays: in fact, East Anglia is the fastest developing region, and Norfolk with Norwich, more attractive to tourists and people in retirement; and Norfolk has an excellent climate, dry and sunny for much of the year, with no worse winters, and with winter days like this, of exhilarating freshness and sunshine.

LONG LIVE NORFOLK!

Fred Pratt Green: *Diary 1987*, after over 17 happy years in Norwich

Over the years, Fred was to establish many contacts in the area. Owen Waters gained a place in his poetry cycle *Ten Friends.*

The Greens' garden

Happisburgh, Norfolk, a painting by Owen Waters.
The original was in the Greens' Norwich home.

70

OWEN WATERS

When we moved into your landscape
you were just a friend of a friend,
except that to be an artist
is to become a legend.

It was months before we met.
You were soft-spoken, neat,
defensively-bearded, ready
to beat a retreat.

You let us see your paintings;
they were strictly representational,
in your own Norfolk tradition,
and very professional.

O most orderly of artists
(every painting photographed
and filed), I warmed to you,
and would have laughed

if I had known you longer,
for I, too, am organized.
Passing into your music-room
I was more surprised.

Arranged in meticulous order
were tapes, records, biographies,
with the very latest equipment,
demanding expertise.

What remarkable versatility!
Such a wide-ranging intellect
is more than a friend of a friend
has a right to expect.

Musically, I am not someone
whose judgement you can rely on:
do you remember I fell asleep
during Havergal Brian,

missing an entire movement,
and may even have snored?
Smiling, you said I was not the first
Brian had bored.

So typical of your courtesy!
It helps me to understand
why I cannot imagine you
with a gun in your hand;

and why you, and our mutual friend
(bird-watching in Brighton town)
were young pacifists together
in the Hitler showdown.

Your reserve, though not a barrier
to immediate communication,
not a thorn-hedge or brick wall,
signals a concentration,

perhaps; a need for privacy
in a chatterbox age
which has substituted videos
for the printed page.

And sometimes I think I sense
beneath your kindness, your charm,
your tranquillity, the echoes
of persistent alarm.

Instinctively, we do not press
our relationship too hard,
which maybe is why it survives
so fresh and unscarred.

Fred Pratt Green: *Ten Friends: O.W.*

Owen and Rita Waters at Fred's eightieth birthday party

JOHN WILSON

In earlier days here, when I was in good walking form, I used to go, on most fine days, for a walk that took me down Thunder Lane to the railway, then over the bridge by the River Yare. There were several possibilities: a shorter walk to the bend of the river and then home the same way, or a round walk, round the marshes following the river path until it turns away, and it is possible to find the path that ultimately brings you back to the railway bridge. How I loved these walks, almost always alone. You might see a heron; once a kingfisher flashed past me; mallards and swans shared the river with boats of various kinds, even sometimes a small tramp boat making for the port (!) of Norwich...I remember how I picnicked on the other side of the Yare – going by car – and wrote 'For the fruits of his creation'. I often took a draft of a hymn with me on these walks.

Fred Pratt Green: *Diary 1987.* It was for Francis Jackson's tune EAST ACKLAM that John Wilson asked Fred to write the Harvest Hymn.

Fred's hymns published in 1969 were written to order, and that was to be the pattern of almost all of the texts produced in the 1970s. John Wilson and Erik Routley, the fifth and sixth of the especially benign influences in Fred's life, supplied the initial stimulus to the writing of many of the hymns created in the coming decade. But for them, it is almost certain that several masterpieces emerging during that period would not have been conceived.

John Wilson was a member of the *Hymns and Songs* committee and was the first to recognise the full extent of Fred's potential as a hymn-writer. John fed Fred with tunes, especially those which he wished to air at his annual *Come and Sing* sessions in Westminster Abbey, or at the yearly conferences of The Hymn Society of Great Britain and Ireland, of which he was a founder-member. He led Fred to join the Society and meet a wide range of others interested in hymnody.

John Wilson, a member of both the Methodist Church and Anglican Communion, became not only a firm friend but also a trusted mentor. Fred sent the drafts of his hymns to John for valued criticism: and a number went through several drafts before Fred was satisfied with his work. These exchanges between John and Fred are all recorded by Fred among numerous other mementoes in 51 scrapbooks, of which the originals are housed at Emory University in Atlanta. A beautifully copied set may be found in the Pratt Green Collection at the University of Durham, England.

Our thanks to all who taught us what we know
of Hymnody: the valued critic who
encourages a latent gift to grow,
and wields a pretty pruning-knife; the true
and truthful friend who, lacking expertise,
has insights of his own; the editor
who takes a risk or troubles to advise,
firmly believing this is what he's for;
reviewers who review not to destroy
but to evaluate; musicians keen
to help a congregation to enjoy
a new experience in an old routine;
and those who say they love the old hymns best,
yet sing the new with lively interest.

Fred Pratt Green: *Sonnet for John Wilson*

John Wilson (1905–1992)

ERIK ROUTLEY

In the decades following the Second World War, nobody did more than Erik Routley (1917–1982) by his many books and his personal contacts to create a new enthusiasm for hymns and all things concerning them.

In the early seventies, Erik was preparing the international ecumenical hymn book *Cantate Domino*, and he invited Fred to pen several English translations of texts by Edmund Budry, Jochen Klepper, Dominique Ombrie, Frederico Pagura, Didier Rimaud, Claude Rozier, Kurt Rummel, Paulus Stein and the compilation by Otto Riethmuller of the German of Christian David, Christian Gottlob Barth and Christian Gottleb. In many instances, the hymns were for simultaneous singing in more than one language, and they tested Fred's abilities to overcome many technical difficulties. The new translation of Budry's text was needed because *Thine be the glory, risen conquering son* was not sufficiently near to the author's original. Though Fred was no linguist, he was able to work with literal English translations of the foreign-language texts. When Erik went to work at Princeton, he played a significant role in introducing Fred to the United States.

In May 1979 Erik Routley published *An English-speaking Hymnal Guide*. This substantial book gathered together the most memorable hymns in the English language, with an introduction on the subject and notes on each hymn and its author. Contemporary hymn-writers were mostly represented by one hymn, generally their best-known and most widely published. In my case, it was *Christ is the world's light*.

But the book carried a dedication. It certainly gave me a shock:

> To
>
> FREDERICK PRATT GREEN
>
> in whom the genius of Charles Wesley
>
> lives again

While I was grateful for such an ascription, I was also a little upset. I felt that to compare me with Charles Wesley was calculated to do me more harm than good! What am I but a mouse to the Wesley elephant? Erik's enthusiasm had surely gone too far. So I wrote a sonnet: 'To Dr Erik Routley on Receiving from him a most excellent book of his own Authorship and bearing this kindly Dedication: To........'

I think it worth transcribing the octet:

You honour me, dear friend, beyond my right.
Stand, I more than others, in the shade
Of Wesley's genius, more than half afraid
To risk exposure to so strong a light;
For mine's a timely talent, much too slight
To wear the laurels that can never fade,
And satisfied sometimes to make the grade
By keeping Watts and Wesley just in sight.

I think this expresses my own estimate of my contribution to hymnody in relation to the immense contribution of Charles Wesley. I went on, in the playful sonnet, to compare Watts and Wesley (I myself am a Watts man):

Which is the greater? Charles's inward eye?
Or Isaac's vision of the universe?
(Let punters argue who has won the purse:
A photo finish proves there is a tie!)

Courtesy demanded more than this. And, in spite of my doubts of Erik's wisdom and sane judgement, I was also pleased (who wouldn't be?):

How can I thank you, friend? Your reckless praise
Makes this, I do confess, my day of days!

Fred Pratt Green: from the unpublished *Notes of a Hymn Writer*, written in 1980

ALAN WEBSTER

Very few proven facts are known about Mother Julian, the English mystic, save that on 8 May 1373 and on the following day she received a series of visions, which she set down as the *Revelations of Divine Love*, issued 20 years later. This book seeks to provide clues to all the problems of existence, including that of the existence of evil.

The Cathedral of the Holy and Undivided Trinity at Norwich was founded in the twelfth century as a monastic church under the Benedictine Rule. Mother Julian, also known as the Lady Julian, was probably an anchoress, a person who not only withdraws from the world to live a solitary life of silence, prayer and mortification, but who chooses to live in closely confined quarters. Around the year 1200, an unidentified author in the West Midlands wrote a Rule for Anchoresses for a group of recluses living locally, the *Ancren(e) Riwle* or *Ancrene Wisse*. That rule included an instruction: 'Ye shall not possess any beast, my dear sister, except only a cat.'

Although there is no evidence that Mother Julian actually took advantage of a cat as permitted company, the stained glass Julian Window in the cathedral pictures the creature.

The year 1973 brought me an exceptional opportunity… Great celebrations marked this Anniversary of Mother Julian's vision with services in the cathedral, the new Roman Catholic cathedral and elsewhere, with an ecumenical Eucharist on Saturday 5th May at 12 noon. For these celebrations, I was commissioned by the Dean and the ecumenical committee, to write two processional hymns, for the entrance and exit of the clergy, one rather general, the other specifically about Julian. Since I knew almost nothing, beyond the barest facts, about Mother Julian and her famous book, I had to do quite an amount of reading and research. Perhaps no task was to give me greater pleasure than this. I owe it, of course to Alan Webster, who was to give me further opportunities…

Fred Pratt Green: from the unpublished *Notes of a Hymn Writer*, written in 1980

One of these was to be the commission, also for Norwich Cathedral, of a hymn to celebrate the Queen's Silver Jubilee, which subsequently was adopted in the official Order of Service agreed by representatives of all the Churches. It was sung in churches up and down the land and in many parts of the Commonwealth, and the media made much of the fact that it had ousted the Poet Laureate's poem for the occasion, causing Fred real distress at the time as Sir John Betjeman had given him much encouragement in his early poetry writing.

The Very Revd Alan Webster, Dean of Norwich, with Fred

JULIAN OF NORWICH

The hymns Fred wrote are still sung in Julian circles today, and one that he adapted in 1977 as a general hymn, *Rejoice in God's saints, today and all days*, has gained wider currency. Quoted here for interest, however, is the original version, dating from 1973. Subsequently, Fred received many commissions for hymns relating to various saints both familiar and obscure, and a fascinating programme could be assembled from them on the theme of 'A celebration of many saints'. Fred also wrote a poem, *Mother Julian's Cat*, which he dedicated to the Dean of Norwich. Characteristically, it is both funny and serious: an excellent example of his use of humour as a tool of his ministry. In defence of the use of this imaginary story, if ecclesiastics can permit such a liberty as a cat in a stained glass window, why not poets?

Rejoice in God's saints
This day of all days!
A world without saints
Forgets how to praise!
Rejoice in their courage,
Their spiritual skill;
In Julian of Norwich
Rejoice, all who will!

The candle she lit
Six centuries gone,
By darkness beset
Shines quietly on.
Her cell is no prison,
Though narrow and dim,
For Jesus is risen,
And she lives in him.

How bright in her cell
The showings of God!
No writings could tell
What love understood.
She suffers his Passion,
She grieves over sin;
She knows his compassion
Has made us all kin.

How courteous is God!
All love and all light!
In God's Motherhood
She finds her delight.
She pleads for the sinner,
She wrestles with Hell;
God answers: *All manner*
Of things shall be well!

Dear Lord, we would learn
To walk in this way,
With patience discern
How best to obey
That call to perfection
You taught us to face:
Lord, fix our direction,
And keep us in grace.

Fred Pratt Green:
In Commemoration of Julian of Norwich

I

Of all who come to pay respect
To our world-famous saint,
How many cry: 'She's got a cat!'
And think it cute or quaint.

Bemused by overmuch, they peer
At Julian and her cat;
But rarely is there any doubt
What they are looking at.

So, ill at ease with sanctity,
They give the cat a smile,
And suddenly are quite at home
In our historic pile:

For anchorites and anchoresses
Seem less remote and odd
Because a woman loved her cat
While giving all to God.

II

How Lady Julian got her cat
Is left with me to tell.
It happened, like a miracle,
The day she got her cell.

While Holy Church, in panoply,
Effected her enclosure,
A cat stole in, and washed herself
With elegant composure.

At this the people mentioned Ah!
In homely admiration,
And even some religious lost
Their perfect concentration.

And several caitiffs in the crowd
Broke into loud applause,
As, unimpressed by Holy Church,
The creature licked her paws.

continued on next page

III

But would the Hierarchy permit
A cat's participation
In what the Bishop pointed out
Was still a top vocation?

The Bishop's chaplain, zealously,
Whispered the information
That Satan, in the guise of cat,
Could work the soul's damnation;

That anchorites must crucify
Each creaturely emotion;
That cats notoriously exact
An absolute devotion.

Let theologians fight like cats,
Then seek the Pope's advice –
A cat's vocation, Lollards said,
Is keeping down the mice!

IV

But Julian gazed upon the cat
With a benign expression.
'Do you not know the ancient Rule
That guardeth our profession?

'My Lord,' she said submissively,
'Our Rule doth not allow
An anchoress, for earthly gains
To keep a milking cow;

Nor shall she harbour any beast
Save only one – a cat;
And this the good God giveth me
To share my cell.' Whereat

The cat rolled over playfully,
For petting nothing loth;
Whereat the Bishop blessed the cat,
And then enclosed them both.

V

So Julian in her anchorage
Began her life's vocation,
For her enclosure, be it said,
Was not incarceration,

But living in a little space
To give the soul more room
To manifest that state of grace
When revelations come.

In all she suffered, all she found
Of spiritual delight,
She had a cat for company,
As any spinster might.

The cat went in and out at will,
By morning, noon, and night,
Pursuing her instinctive needs,
As any mouser might.

VI

It wasn't long before the cat
When hunting in God's house,
Captured, with expert cruelty,
An inoffensive mouse.

Smugly she laid her offering
On Lady Julian's mat.
Alas, a mouse must be a mouse,
A cat must be a cat!

There is a day for every saint
Of God-accusing grief,
When anti-revelation strains
The back-bone of belief;

When saints, so very vulnerable
To God's upsetting ways,
Must meekly offer up in prayer
The thing they cannot praise.

VII

Yet we may confidently claim
That Julian in her cat
Found cause for much hilarity,
And much to wonder at.

Maybe she dropt her hazel nut
To see her cat play ball
As cheekily as any boy
Against a convent wall;

Maybe, after a running fight
With doubt and accidie,
She called the Devil's bluff and took
The cat upon her knee;

Maybe that soft accompaniment,
That engine under fur,
Added to silence quietude.
If only saints could purr!

VIII

Was Julian's cat, we speculate,
A Tabitha or Tom?
And what its breed? Unhappily,
We cannot argue from

A stained-glass image or a line
In some ambiguous Rule.
They leave the options open. So,
Wanting to play it cool,

MOTHER JULIAN'S CAT

I have assumed, dear Dean, a she
As somewhat more discreet,
The cat had kittens then! for this
Surely is right and meet.

So Julian, moved by kitten-care,
More deeply understood
The nature of our Father-God
And blessed his Motherhood.

IX

A purring cat, a praying saint,
Is just as it should be,
A purring saint, a praying cat –
That is eccentricity!

Yet purring is a giving thanks,
Mewing a trustful prayer,
As any saint who keeps a cat
Will lovingly declare.

But cats that mew extremely loud
Insist on their own way;
And it is sometimes true of us
That this is why we pray.

Julian, with cat for company,
You taught yourself to pray
In everything, for Jesu's love,
Benedicite Domine!

Mother Julian Window (Right),
Norwich Cathedral

Fred Pratt Green: *Mother Julian's Cat*. The poem is dedicated to the Very Revd Alan Webster.

A small part of the wide range of subjects on which Fred wrote hymns and ballads in his retirement years is shown in the snippets reproduced here. The full hymn texts are available in the volumes *The Hymns and Ballads of Fred Pratt Green* and *Later Hymns and Ballads and Fifty Poems*. Almost all are also available in Great Britain and Ireland on the *HymnQuest* CD-ROM. (See page ii). It is hoped that the following excerpts will encourage an exploration of the full texts.

THE LOVE OF MONEY

What authority he wields!
With a whip of cords he clears
Temple courts of profiteers!

All is ready for the Feast!

Casual despoilers, or high-priests of Mammon,
selling the future for present rewards.
Careless of life and contemptuous of beauty:
bid them remember: the Earth is the Lord's.

God in such love for us lent us this planet
(Optional verse)

GOD'S LOVE

For the wonders that astound us,
for the truths that still confound us,
most of all that love has found us,
thanks be to God.

For the fruits of all creation

What to believe? We watch, we listen;
blinded by love, we see
the inexplicable is simple –
You died for me!

What have you done to die in anguish?

77

A WIDE RANGE OF SUBJECTS...

FAITH

But if the thing I most desire
is not your way for me,
may faith, when tested in the fire,
prove its integrity.

Here, Master, in this quiet place

THE HOLY SPIRIT

Only the Spirit's power
can fit us for this hour:
come, Holy Spirit, come!
Instruct, inspire, unite;
and make us see the light:
come, Holy Spirit, come!

Let every Christian pray

Come, Holy Spirit, aid us
to keep the vows we make,
this very day invade us,
and every bondage break.
Come, give our life direction,
the gift we covet most:
to share the resurrection
that leads to Pentecost.

When Jesus came to Jordan

THE DARK NIGHT OF THE SOUL

God does not ask our faithful Love,
then leave us in despair,
when life's misfortunes seem to prove
there is no God to care:
but gives us Hope to steady Faith,
and in our grief restore
Love's confidence that even death
is but an opening door.

Though Love is greatest of the three

When our confidence is shaken
in beliefs we thought secure;
when the spirit in its sickness
seeks but cannot find a cure:
God is active in the tensions
of a faith not yet mature.

When our confidence is shaken

MUSIC

For all who make music for love of the Gospel

For each kind of music that adds a dimension

FEAR OF THE NEW

May God protect his people now
from fear of all things new,
and teach us to discriminate
between the false and true;
and show us, for the gospel's sake,
what we must think and do.

God bless us all who at this time

FORGIVENESS

We must forgive your brother:
he's done the work of two,
but never tried to smother
his envy, son, of you.
Why should he be the loser,
because the lost is found?
Let there be songs and dancing,
and pass the love-cup round!

All of you share my gladness

SHARING

God it is who gives us bread.
God who gives us beauty;
God it is who for our good
lays on us this duty –
Earth is his, and earth is ours,
given to us for sharing;
share the Master's love of flowers,
share his work of caring.

Praise the Lord for all delights

HUMAN UNIQUENESS

What joy it is to worship here,
and find ourselves at home,
where God, who uses every gift,
has room for all who come!
Yet are no two of us alike
of all the human race,
and we must seek a common ground
if we would share his grace.

What joy it is to worship here

HUMAN RIGHTS

Pray for Christ's dissidents, who daily wait,
as Jesus waited in the olive grove,
the unjust trial, the pre-determined fate,
the world's contempt for reconciling love.
Shall all they won for us, at such a cost,
be by our negligence or weakness lost?

Pray for the Church, afflicted and oppressed

...FOR A WIDE RANGE OF OCCASIONS

DEEDS OF HORROR

Dying Lord, what deeds of horror
done for you, stain history's page!
Make us heed this woman's* warning
to her own and every age:
God is God! we cannot threaten
or persuade him to fulfil
not his loving, flawless purpose
but our blind and blunted will.

Praise the God of our salvation
The woman is the apocryphal Judith

THE SECULAR WORLD

Make us, O Christ the ministers
of all you have to give,
until at last the nations learn
the truths by which we live.

Then science shall be sacrament,
as love insists it should,
and all things secular conspire
To serve the greatest good.

Man cannot live by bread alone

PRAISE

Lord, your unbelievers praise you
in their love of humankind:
for there's nothing worth achieving
lies outside your loving mind.
So shall scientists acclaim you
seeing cause where some see chance;
trusting in their dark researches
that your universe makes sense.

Lord, you do not need our praises

WORLD RELIGIONS

Finding in dialogue with other creeds
our faith in Christ confirmed and purified.

Come, share with us as every Christian can

SILENCE

Deeper than our rejoicing,
our praises and our praying,
in an unbroken silence
your inner voice is heard.

Alone, or brought together,
in praying you prepare us
to give you daily service
in your demanding world.

Daily we come, dear Master

THE SABBATH

And yet, how soon we can destroy
the Sabbath God has given:
to sourness turn our sacred joy,
and make a hell of heaven.
Too strict we lose the right to choose;
too lax our soul's direction lose.

God rested on the Seventh Day

HOLY COMMUNION

And after Supper he washed their feet
for service, too, is sacrament.
In him our joy shall be made complete –
sent out to serve, as he was sent.

An Upper Room did our Lord prepare

ASCENSION

The Lord has ascended – his work is complete!
and theirs has begun who once sat at his feet.

Three years they had known him as Master and Lord

LENT

This is where we make our choices,
each in our own wilderness;
where the wild beasts haunt the shadows,
where the angels stoop to bless.

Forty years the Chosen People

TRAVEL

God be praised! a travelled mind
takes a wider vision home;
prejudice is overcome;
there's still hope for humankind:
Alleluia!

Praise the God whose world this is

THE MEDIA

So may those who mould opinion
help us get our values right,
and the artist's private vision
sharpen our defective sight.

Lord of every art and science

IF YOU DON'T ASK...

Although Fred's carols are less well known than his hymns, they are wide-ranging in their subject matter, and fine examples of how the inspiration of music fuelled his imagination. It is hoped that the inclusion of three of them here will lead to a greater appreciation of their delights. They would form excellent material for a concert, one put on, for example, to celebrate the centenary of his birth in 2003. Such an event need not be confined only to Christmas; Fred preferred the traditional definition of the form to its Victorian variant, and wrote his carols as seasonal songs for both sacred and secular use throughout the year.

Many of them came into being, like his hymns, as the result of individual requests from a myriad of people. Fred always enjoyed responding to these challenges, but two in particular gave him particular pleasure. In 1973, Alan Luff, editor of the Welsh Carol Book *Llyfr Carolau Deiniol*, sent Fred several old carol tunes, to which Welsh poets had written words over the centuries. The request was for English words, perhaps catching the theme of the Welsh, but capturing the elaborate rhyming structure of the original. One of the six, in the Welsh metre *Venture Gwen* is also printed here. The copyright arrangement is by Mansel Thomas. It is published, with two other sets of Fred's words, in *Tair Carol Gymreig (Three Welsh Carols)* by Mansel Thomas Trust Publications.

A few years later, June Boyce-Tillman commended several European carol tunes for the *Galliard Book of Carols*, of which she was a co-editor. This book included carols on both secular and religious themes: in *A Concert-goers' Carol*, to a traditional Basque melody, perhaps he combines both, as it ends, *All good music is the Lord's; but who can say what he applauds?* Other titles include *A Mistletoe Carol* (Dutch 15th century), *A Carol for Christingle* (Czech), *Ring the Bells of Bethlehem!* (French 18th Century), *The Donkey's Carol* (French 12th century), *A Carol for Easter Saturday* (French 16th Century), *Easter Day Carol, A Lovers' Carol* and *Shrove Tuesday Carol* (all three Burgundian).

Angelic hosts proclaimed him
    when he came, when he came,
our Lord and Saviour named him,
    when he came.
As David's town lay dreaming
that night of our redeeming,
how few there were esteemed him,
    when he came, when he came;
poor peasant's child they deemed him,
    when he came.

His love for us has pleaded,
    his alone, his alone,
his sacrifice is needed,
    his alone.
He whose forgiveness freed us
shall by his Spirit lead us
whose flocks are safely feeding,
    his alone, his alone,
no other voices heeding,
    his alone.

All you who need protection,
    come to him, come to him,
against the world's infection,
    come to him;
you who no hope expected,
defeated and dejected:
you who have life rejected,
    come to him, come to him;
himself the Resurrected,
    come to him.

His seed in secret growing,
    everywhere, everywhere,
has now its winter-sowing,
    everywhere.
What love it takes – how slowly! –
to make one sinner holy:
but Christ has for his showing,
    everywhere, everywhere,
harvests beyond our knowing
    everywhere.

Fred Pratt Green: *When he came*, based on themes selected from John Davies' 19-verse hymn

VENTURE GWEN

Bangor MSS 2254, page 18,
arranged Mansel Thomas (1909–1986)

Mesur : Mentra Gwen
Melody : Venture Gwen

Melody: Bangor MSS 2254, p. 18

Penillion Cymraeg 2 a 4 (yr alaw gan y tenor)
English Verses 2 & 3 (melody in the tenor)

FAUXBOURDON

A CONCERT-GOERS' CAROL

Fred Pratt Green (1903–2000)

Traditional Basque
Arranged Allen Percival (1925–1992)

This carol may be sung by SA, SAB or SATB with or without keyboard or guitar (in the key of G).

o can measure
mpart?
ded pleasure
d and heart.

us.
f delight
rs grant us:

ord's,

Turo, luro, luro, what a rondo!
What a strange, exciting beat!
How its final grand crescendo
Gets us tapping with our feet!
Relaxed, at ease,
And quiet, please,
Good people all,
Who fill this hall,
Discover, discover
No one has to read the score
To become a music-lover.
None shall name us
Ignoramus
If our pleasure is sincere,
And makes us want
To stand and cheer.

o, luro, luro, brave conductor,
kling something new and hard;
nust know it tastes like nectar
to the avant-garde.
at you hear
s the ear,
t the noise
ear the voice
son, of reason:
lispleases you tonight,
ay learn to love next season!
lisasters
t masters,
music is the Lord's;
can say
applauds?

reen

Bars 1–5 of A Concert-Goers' Carol, page 82, should read as follows:

ERRATUM

Fred Pratt Green (1903–2000)

Traditional Basque
Arranged Allen Percival (1925–1992)

Turo, luro, luro, luro,
Relaxed, at ease, and quiet, please
Discover, discover!
Become a music lover.
None shall name us Ignoramus
It makes us want to stand and cheer.

o, luro,
ar insults the ear
reason
...ay well love next season!
Some disasters turn out masters.
But who can say what he applauds?

THE OXFORD HYMNODY CONFERENCE

The International Hymnody Conference held at Oxford in August 1981, which brought together the main streams of British, American and European hymnody, was the catalyst that turned Fred from an emerging British hymn-writer to one known and loved worldwide. Fred begins the story in his unpublished *Notes of a Hymn Writer*:

Another surprise! A few weeks before the Oxford Conference I received a letter from Hope Publishing Company saying that they would like to publish a complete anthology of my hymns, providing they could secure control of copyright in the States and Canada…About the same time – but with no collusion, Bernard Braley of Stainer & Bell expressed in more general terms much the same interest. The obvious thing was to bring the two proposers together! And in no time an agreement was reached – cemented at the Oxford Conference – that Stainer & Bell should go ahead preparing a book of about 256 pages, with 200 or so texts, each with background information and comments taken from my Scrapbooks, with a preface (? by Erik Routley), introductions by Bernard (as editor) and myself, with indexes, and ILLUSTRATIONS(!). The Hope Publishing Company would control copyright in the USA & Canada, Stainer & Bell in the 'rest of the world'…

All this has meant a renewal of my close contacts with Bernard (in connection with *Partners in Praise* and *The Galliard Book of Carols*). A great deal of correspondence followed, with two long and laborious week-ends at East Finchley. Many small problems arose…But Bernard is an organising genius, and by the middle of December the main body of the book was ready for printing by Bernard's Galliard factory in Great Yarmouth.

It is proposed to send a film of the book to America, where it will be separately printed and published, in time it is hoped, for the 60th anniversary of the Hymn Society of America at Atlanta in June 1982. I am invited to be present, as guest, which means flying from Heathrow direct to Atlanta – a seven-hour flight. Quite an adventure ahead, if I am fit enough to go, with Marjorie, of course, who has always said nothing would persuade her to 'go up'! I expect she will change her mind…

Fred Pratt Green: *Notes of a Hymn Writer*

And so to America. The final programme for the Greens included a meeting in Savannah with the veteran American hymn-writer Francis Bland Tucker and the conferring of an honorary doctorate in humane letters by the Methodist foundation, the University of Emory in Atlanta. Fred was awarded the Fellowship of the Hymn Society of America; and the Greens visited the University United Methodist Church at Austin in Texas, who had commissioned a hymn to ABBOT'S LEIGH for which Fred wrote *God is here! As we his people*. Time was also spent at Beaufort, South Carolina and at Point Clear, Alabama. The trip resulted in a host of new contacts and was extremely significant – many of his later hymns were commissions from the United States – and his hymns featured thereafter in numerous American hymn books.

We share, in hymns, a common heritage;
our hymnals look remarkably the same,
with Watts and Wesley centre of the stage.
Your Sacred Songs and Solos put to shame
our formal worship, and your ethnic range
our insularity. Contrariwise, your love
of interlining, growing now less strange,
we think obscures the poetry. The glove
is not a perfect fit. 'Bondage' you ban
as pornographic in Vermont and Texas,
and 'saddle-bag' is rude in Michigan.
So like yet so unlike! and to perplex us
not every hymn crosses the wide Atlantic
without a problem social or semantic!

Fred Pratt Green: *Sonnet for George Shorney*

George Shorney (Head of Hope Publishing Company)
with Fred and Marjorie at Atlanta

The President, Trustees and Faculty
of Emory University

take pleasure in awarding to

FRED PRATT GREEN

the degree of Doctor of Humane Letters

Remarkable minister, man of letters, gifted poet of the Word, you have answered to the Church's need for new songs of love and joy and peace and, in doing so, have replenished our will to courage and to unity. For two decades you have bent your thoughts, your skill, your energies to this important task, wedding words to music with sympathy, elegance and rare proportion. Hearing and singing these compelling hymns, we have begun what our children will continue, appropriating your harvest of song into the common life of the Church. For so blessing our worship with your generous and creative love, Fred Pratt Green, Emory University is honored to salute you this day, in the very spirit of your life and work, ad maiorem Dei gloriam.

President

Given under the Seal of the University in Atlanta, Georgia, on this twentieth day of June, in the Year of Our Lord, nineteen hundred and eighty-two.

Emory University Citation

Fred and Marjorie with the Russell family. The Russells were Ministers of Music at University United Methodist Church, Austin, Texas

VISITORS FROM ABROAD

In the remaining years at their Norwich home, the Greens received a steady stream of overseas visitors. Some brought whole choirs with them to Norwich, and several presented programmes in Chapel Field Methodist Church. Fred was kept busy coping with new commissions for hymns. He was never wholly happy with calls from America to be gender conscious about the nature of God; but he did his best to comply with requests, and theologically fully appreciated that, if male and female were made in God's image, God's nature must comprise the elements we describe in human terms as fatherhood and motherhood. Where people took too extreme a view, however, he let off steam from time to time with poems poking gentle fun.

So, God, we may no longer call you HE,
Because the ladies (bless 'em) are upset
(Oh, not the ladies I've consulted yet),
Insisting you are just as much a SHE,
As all peace-loving, sober males agree.
But wait a minute, ladies, and admit
The very stones cry out that God is IT –
Do they not share God's creativity?

Fairness demands a positive position.
Why not HE, SHE, and IT? Clumsy, you think?
Better to spoil a rhythm than to vex
One single member of the opposite sex;
Shall not HE, SHE, and IT grant absolution,
Being the Ground of Humour, with a wink?

Fred Pratt Green: *Sexism in Hymnody*

I have already written one hymn *In Honour of the Virgin Mary*, commemorating her presence at the Crucifixion. I would not find the Roman Catholic Veneration of Mary a real stumbling block (the Bodily Assumption excepted!). Surely if the New Testament is to be taken as a true record of events, Mary must be given exceptional honour. In this Catholicism has a nice answer to those who demand that the Godhead is not solely 'masculine', that God is our Mother as well as our Father. The God of Protestantism has all too often represented God as a kind of Almighty Puritan Divine. Of course, I can't enter the competition (for a hymn in celebration of the Marian year proclaimed by the Pope). A pity!

Fred Pratt Green: *Diary 1987*

Fred first met Professor Hofmann at the Oxford conference.

A very carefully planned day – following Professor Hofmann's specific wishes – passed off satisfactorily. I had arranged for the party to walk from the Nelson Hotel to the South Door of the Cathedral for an official welcome. The walk by the river and through the close is delightful and only takes about 15 minutes. The morning was gloriously fine. They decided to go by coach! This meant arriving at the wrong door for the welcome, but Marjorie took charge for me, coped valiantly. In the afternoon I had fixed for a City Guide to take them on what is called *The Historical Tour of the City* – on foot and lasting 1¹/₂ hours. I was anxious, knowing how hard it was proving to get the group anywhere on time, about the meeting at the West Door with the Guide – however all was well. (M & I stayed at home.)

Then the chief event: a meeting at Chapel Field, so that we could have a discussion about church life and then a singing by the Germans of German hymns, including several translations of my hymns by Hofmann. We had left the meeting open for anyone who was prepared to stay after Evening Service. We were fortunate in having not only a splendid interpreter in Keith, but the participation of the special preacher of the day, Dr Kenneth Greet, who was an enormous help, explaining the intricacies of the Anglican constitution as the State Church, the relationship of the various denominations, church unity…even finances! There was no lack of questions – and the singing was quite remarkable, especially as no rehearsals were possible.

Fred Pratt Green: *Diary 1987 (A Day to Remember)*

RONALD WATSON

An interesting letter this morning from Ronald Watson, organist of Saint Giles' Church, for which I wrote a hymn on their patron saint entailing research. His letter is appreciative. He wants me to write a carol for a tune he has composed. Nothing would give me greater pleasure – and no doubt some frustration, but there's a snag. The tune, rhythmically, is complex, though it looks simple enough, and at the moment I can't get the hang of it! The question is: shall I ask him to come here and play it to me or get one of my musical friends to come to my aid? Ronald Watson is a stranger – a competent musician obviously. Decided to phone him and fix a meeting.

Fred Pratt Green: *Diary 6 January 1986*

This phone call had a dramatic effect on the rest of Fred's life. He had found a new creative partner. They spurred each other into creativity, meeting for workshop sessions at frequent intervals. Even more important, they became firm friends. Ron does not feature in his poetry cycle *Ten Friends*, but Fred dedicates the cycle to him. 'These prosy poems, all written except the first, in my 88th year, about ten of my friends, six of them dead, and four now living, are dedicated to the friend of my old age, RON WATSON, lecturer and musician.'

A very interesting coffee session with Ron Watson this afternoon. He talked of his early life and how he came to Norwich to lecture on structural engineering at the City College. One thing he said about his life surprised and interested me. All his life, he said, he had had an older man as his friend since they had something to offer him arising out of their longer and different experience of life. This explains how he has found my friendship stimulating, as he has often explained. Ron is a northerner like myself, with all this means in terms of frankness and loyalty. I enjoy his company; feel perfectly at ease with him, appreciate his (northern) type of humour; and of course share his love of music and the arts.

Fred Pratt Green: *Diary 20 November 1987*

Ron was a true friend to Fred through the nineties, providing company and companionship in his last years. Fred had several nieces and nephews, but all were elderly and none lived nearby. Ron acted therefore as a next-of-kin during the last years at Cromwell House and no one could have performed this role more faithfully and lovingly. That their creative partnership seldom yielded published work was more due to the state of the British music publishing market and the abundance of American musicians making anthem and secular choral settings for the buoyant United States market than to the inherent quality of their partnership. Here is the text of just one of Fred's *Sequence of Texts for Saint Valentine* for which Ron provided the music:

Both: Sweetheart, you've been my Valentine
    For all these married years;
    And what was yours and what was mine
    We never needed to define,
    For everything was ours.

He: We've shared, in bright and cloudy days,
    Our laughter and our tears;
    And kept together in life's maze
    When many go their separate ways,
    And even memory sours.

She: And if dark days should bring again
    Anxieties and fears,
    We know the lark will sing again,
    That after Winter, Spring again
    Will fill the world with flowers.

Both: Dear Love, I'll be your Valentine
    Through all the coming years.
    Content to share this life of mine
    With you, and always proudly sign
    Myself: For ever yours!

Fred Pratt Green: *A Duet for Married Lovers*

The Watsons (left) with Victor Green (nephew)
and Phil (his partner)

CROMWELL HOUSE

By 1988, the stream of commissions had slowed to a trickle and the postman did not deliver mail every day. Fred felt the time had come to retire from hymn-writing, although he was kept busy with work on *Later Hymns and Ballads and Fifty Poems*, to be published in 1989. The time was coming for Marjorie and Fred to move into Cromwell House, a retirement home for the elderly run by the charity Methodist Homes for the Aged. Fred relished the prospect but Marjorie was unhappy about the change, with which she never really came to terms. They moved in 1990 and Fred, whose writing days we all thought were over, suddenly blossomed once more in verse. So *The Last Lap*, a sequence of over 50 poems about life in his new environment, was published in 1991 and tells with eloquence, humour and some sadness the trials of old age.

Fred and Marjorie celebrate their last Christmas together

I cannot believe my eyes!
She emerged from her room
backwards. Yes! backwards
in her versatile wheel-chair,
into the long corridor
I have nicknamed The Strand;
then, letting the door gently fall to
she turned the corner, backwards,
and skilfully using the handrails
propelled herself at high speed
to the obliging lift,
enjoying her athleticism.
'Madam,' I said, 'I arrest you
for breaking the speed-limit
in a built-up area, and
for driving a vehicle in reverse,
without a proper licence,
to the danger of the public!'
Of course, what I meant was:
'I award you a gold medal
for courage in overcoming disability,
for making progress backwards,
and for a special kind of humour.'

Fred Pratt Green: *Progress Backwards*

When old age robs us of our dignity,
when under stress of age affections fray,
when wrinkled features threaten to betray
a self less kind, or dread disease sets free
an alien, uncontrolled identity:
I will not look! I turn my face away!
I hate the God, to whom I have to pray,
for doing things like this to you and me.

'Hold on!' cries God, who has another Job
upon his hands: 'How can you hope to probe
the mysteries of my unique creation?
This is the final test, the last temptation,
to lose your grip on My integrity.'
I yield! His word is good enough for me.

Fred Pratt Green: *God answers Job*

In August 1991, Fred and Marjorie celebrated their diamond wedding. At the end of the following year, they spent their last Christmas together, as Marjorie was suffering from cancer of the pancreas. She was tenderly cared for by the staff at Cromwell House, but died on 7 August 1993, shortly after their 62nd wedding anniversary.

FINAL EARTHLY HONOURS

On 2 August 1994, Fred was honoured by Queen and nation with the award of the M.B.E. for his services to hymn-writing. By his choice, he elected not to go to Buckingham Palace, but for the investiture to be undertaken on the sovereign's behalf by the Lord Lieutenant of Norfolk amongst a small group of friends and his fellow residents at Cromwell House.

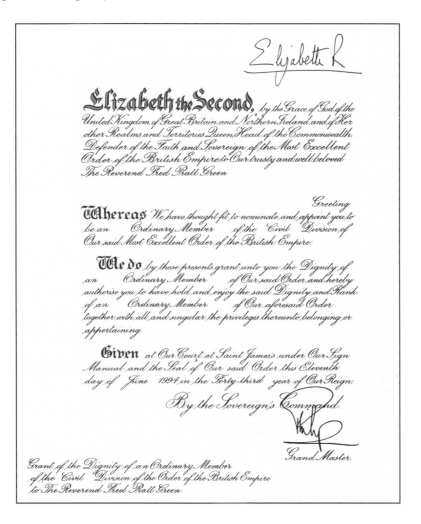

Fred receiving the M.B.E. from
The Lord Lieutenant of Norfolk

Captioned by Fred:
With Jean our wonderful Cook

EPILOGUE

The funeral service for Frederick Pratt Green took place at Chapel Field Road Methodist Church, Norwich, with committal at Earlham Crematorium. In January, his ashes were scattered beneath a tree beloved by both Fred (Derrick) and Marjorie in the grounds of Cromwell House. At each of these three ceremonies, Rev. Michael R. Corney officiated with considerable sensitivity.

Two Methodist colleagues, the District Chair, Rev. Malcolm Braddy (appreciation) and the Circuit Superintendent, Rev. Alan Cox (New Testament lesson) assisted. Five lay persons took particular parts: Ronald Watson (organist), Ray Lucas (epistle), Bernard Braley (appreciation), Elizabeth Shepherd (recorded message and poems) and Victor Green, nephew (poem read in thanksgiving for love and care at Cromwell House). There were four hymns in the Chapel Field service. Fred had chosen *Now thank we all our God* and Wesley's *Son of God, if thy free grace*: the minister and two executors jointly chose two of Fred's hymns: *An Upper Room did our Lord prepare* and *The Church of Christ in every age*. At the Committal, Michael Corney read Fred's little known text entitled *The Future Life*. At the scattering of the ashes, Fred's poem *Eternity* was read.

Son of God, if thy free grace
Again has raised me up,
Called me still to seek thy face,
And given me back my hope:
Still thy timely help afford,
And all thy loving-kindness show:
Keep me, keep me, gracious Lord,
And never let me go!

By me, O my Saviour, stand
In sore temptation's hour;
Save me with thine outstretched hand,
And show forth all thy power;
O be mindful of thy word,
Thy all-sufficient grace bestow:
Keep me, keep me, gracious Lord,
And never let me go!

Give me, Lord, a holy fear,
And fix it in my heart,
That I may from evil near
With timely care depart;
Sin be more than hell abhorred;
Till thou destroy the tyrant foe,
Keep me, keep me, gracious Lord,
And never let me go!

Never let me leave thy breast,
From thee, my Saviour, stray;
Thou art my support and rest,
My true and living way;
My exceeding great reward,
In heav'n above and earth below:
Keep me, keep me, gracious Lord,
And never let me go!

Charles Wesley (1707–1788)

Rest in peace, earth's journey ended,
You whom Christ redeemed, defended:
To the place where saints are one
Safely brought by him alone –
May he grant us like protection –
Rest in peace, earth's journey ended.

Happy soul, to Christ united,
Calmer now and clearer-sighted:
Your new journey now begins,
Freed from earth's besetting sins:
Pressing on towards perfection
Happy soul, to Christ united.

May we meet, dear Lord, in heaven,
Each forgiving, each forgiven,
Each more gifted to pursue
All you have for us to do.
By your Spirit's sure direction
May we meet, dear Lord, in heaven.

Fred Pratt Green: *The Future Life*

Lord, when you promise me Eternity
as fit reward for faithfulness in Time,
the fear that I must always live with me
clouds my imagination. In my prime
I never escaped my shadow; in old age
I find some comfort in oblivion
that puts an end to this tough pilgrimage:
what troubles me is having to live on.

Then faith renews its function to fulfil
what you intend for me; and I desire,
but deeper down than my enfeebled will,
to know the God who is refining fire.
My body burned, is it some other me
your love releases into Eternity?

Fred Pratt Green: *Eternity*

A FINANCIAL LEGACY

Fred was quite clear that it was right and proper that hymn-writers should receive royalties for their work. A labourer in any occupation is entitled to a reward. Christian ministers usually receive stipends, and authors of Christian books receive royalties; he believed hymn-writers and composers should be similarly treated. Initially, his small royalties enabled him to take friends out for a pub lunch; as they unexpectedly blossomed, he purchased joint life and survivor annuities to supplement his small family income as a retired minister. As royalties grew further, he provided support for the Hymn Society of Great Britain and Ireland and the Methodist Church Music Society. The prospect was of much larger royalties in the future, and in 1984 Fred set up a charitable trust for the benefit of hymnody and church music, which would receive his royalties for the full duration of the copyrights. Just two of the imaginative projects undertaken by the Trust are mentioned here. First J. R. Watson describes The Pratt Green Hymnology Collection at the University of Durham.

It was in 1985 that the Trustees sent round an exploratory letter, inviting suggestions and ideas which would enable the Trust to fulfil its principal aim of furthering the cause of hymnody. When I received it, I quickly realized that there were many ways of doing that, but I thought that some of them, such as scholarships, grants to research students and essay prizes, were inevitably connected with a single recipient, and necessarily short-term in their effects. I was searching for a project which would be a permanent resource for the study of hymnology; and in addition I was looking for something which I hoped would raise the status of the subject in the academic world.

After some discussion with the Library staff at the University, therefore, I wrote to suggest that one of the ways of encouraging the cause of hymnody would be to provide a resource for its serious study, and that what was needed, as a first step, was a place where scholars could come and find a wide range of material relating to hymns: hymn books, journals, critical books on hymns, music, hymn book companions, indexes (this was long before the days of *HymnQuest*), facsimiles, biographies, and last, but not least, unpublished material related to hymns and hymn-writers. I hoped that this would be lodged in the library of a well-known university. Durham seemed a natural location. The University had been set up by the Church and retained firm and historic links with it; there were strong departments of English, Theology and a great deal of good will from those sources; and the Cathedral Library, and that of Ushaw College, would provide additional and complementary resources.

The Trustees supported the proposal. The Collection was formally opened by Fred Pratt Green himself on 15 October 1987, in the presence of senior officers of the University. I had driven Fred up from Norwich on the previous day, and I deliberately chose to go over the Humber Bridge, because I knew that he would enjoy a traverse of the York and Hull Methodist District. The journey sparked off many reminiscences about the towns and villages we passed through: 'Closed a chapel there – you should have heard what they said to me', or 'That was where a woman said "we don't want you southerners coming and telling us what to do"; "Madam", I protested mildly, "I was born in Lancashire"; "Just as bad", she said; "we don't want Lancastrians either."'

Opening Ceremony of The Pratt Green Hymnology Collection at the University of Durham. (Left to Right) Richard Watson, Fred (now Sir Fred) Holliday (Vice Chancellor), Fred Pratt Green, Bernard Braley (who presented on behalf of the Trust a double portrait of Fred which has hung beside the Collection to this day).

continued on next page

THE PRATT GREEN HYMNOLOGY COLLECTION

The Oxford University Press kindly donated a copy of the modern edition of the 1780 *Collection of Hymns for the Use of People called Methodists*, edited by Franz Hildebrandt and Oliver Beckerlegge. That donation was the first of many. It was always my hope that the Pratt Green Collection would grow through donation and benefaction. There has been a wonderful response over the years from many people, including authors and publishers, and those who have given treasured volumes and cherished family possessions. Other donors have picked up hymn books at sales, and thought of us; others have saved books that were being thrown away by people who no longer had a use for them. Some donors have been consistent and friendly over many years, showing a real interest and enthusiasm. It is hard to single some out, but a few must be mentioned here. The first was Fred Pratt Green himself, who gave us many of the first hundred volumes from his shelves in Hillcrest Road; then there was Gillian Warr, daughter of Percy Dearmer, who gave us annotated copies of the *English Hymnal*, *Songs of Praise* and *The Oxford Book of Carols*. Other major early benefactors were W. R. Heatley, of Coventry, who had a collection of over 300 items, meticulously annotated and Patrick Morison, who had a special interest in Roman Catholic hymnody, Gregorian Chant, and Plainsong. The Hymn Society of America gave us duplicate copies from its library; and Dr Russell Schulz-Widmar and the Choir of University United Methodist Church at Austin, Texas, sent a generous donation.

Particular items of interest which have arrived since 1987 include the working papers of John Wilson, Fred's great friend and encourager, which had been lovingly assembled and catalogued by his son Anthony Wilson: and photocopies of the original 51 scrapbooks which Fred himself kept as a record of his hymn writing. The originals were promised to Emory University at Atlanta; for scholars on this side of the Atlantic they were scrupulously and faithfully copied for the Durham archive by Roland Buggey. Anyone who thinks that photocopying is an assembling of smudgy black-and-white images should inspect these marvellous copies, which reproduce the original paper colours, ink colours, and exact sizes. The collection also holds copies of some of the plays which Fred wrote in the 1920s and 30s: *Sons of Daybreak Street*, *Farley Goes Out*, *Emancipation*, *The House at Arrow Ghyll*, and *Nursery Farm*. It also has copies of the four volumes of poetry, one of which, *This Unlikely Earth*, is very scarce.

Among important resources for the student of hymnody are the four volumes of Nicholas Temperley's massive *Hymn Tune Index*; a complete run of *The Bulletin of the Hymn Society of Great Britain and Ireland*; partial sets of *The Hymn* and of the *Jarbuch für Liturgik und Hymnologie*; and the CD-ROM *HymnQuest*. Other treasures include some early tune books (William Tans'ur, Thomas Hawkes, Thomas Clark) and eighteenth-century editions of Wesley and Watts; an early edition of John Wesley's *Sacred Harmony*; and a massive representation of nineteenth-century hymnody, both in tune books such as *The Chorale Book for England* and S. S. Wesley's *The European Psalmist*, and in words and tune books of every Christian denominaton (including the Muggletonians). But it must not be thought that the collection is primarily concerned with older hymns: there is a substantial archive of modern hymn books, recently increased on a massive scale by a generous donation of the books from the Oxford University Press hymn department. This benefaction will increase the number of volumes in the collection to around 3,000.

The collection has been widely used by visiting scholars from as far north as Aberdeen and St Andrews, and by others who have been visiting the north east of England. It has been a particular pleasure to welcome authors such as Lionel Adey and Ian Bradley. Three candidates for Durham higher degrees have worked extensively with the collection: Dr Maureen Harris, Dr Margaret Leask, and the Revd Andrew Pratt. Dr Harris did remarkable work in recovering poems that Fred thought he had published, but could not find, by combing the back numbers of such publications as *John o' London's Weekly* and *The New Yorker*. Andrew Pratt worked on the hymns of F. W. Faber, and on the representation of the Four Last Things; and Dr Leake's thesis on 'The Development of English-Language Hymnody and its Use in Worship, 1960-1965' would have delighted Fred himself because of its meticulous and sympathetic survey of the developments in his own time. Finally, without wishing to appear too much a beneficiary of my own initiative, I should add that The *English Hymn* (which I began in 1989, partly as a consequence of the new collection) and the forthcoming Oxford *Anthology of Hymns* would have been infinitely more difficult, if not impossible, without the collection.

continued on next page

HYMNQUEST

It has moved several times, but stayed within the same building, which is the old University Library on Palace Green, in the shadow of the great cathedral. It is now appropriately shelved alongside Music, on open shelves (apart from the irreplaceable items); it is properly catalogued, and is now on the computer, which means it can be accessed by anyone through the Durham University web-site (www. durham.ac.uk/Library). All this has required a great deal of support and hard work, and I would end by recording my grateful thanks to Beth Rainey, the Sub-Librarian in charge of Special Collections, and her staff. Miss Rainey has been invariably supportive and enthusiastic; and special thanks must also go to Sheila Doyle, who has looked after the day-to-day running of the collection, and organised the cataloguing and conservation of the material. But they, and I, could have done little without the continued support and generosity of The Pratt Green Trust, which has created at Durham an archive and study centre which is worthy of the hymn-writer in whose honour it was named. Sometimes, as I browse among its shelves, I think – *si monumentum requiris, circumspice*.

Richard Watson: *The Pratt Green Hymnology Collection at the University of Durham*

The *HymnQuest* CD-ROM, published in May 2000 and already updated in January 2001, is the culmination of several Trust initiatives over a period of nine years. One of these had already succeeded in persuading many more churches to respect copyright law. This stood the Trust in good stead when it was seeking the permission to publish the CD-ROM.

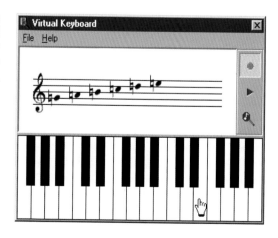

The CD-ROM includes 25,300 first lines (including many choruses), 15,000 full texts, 98,000 links to 2,000 different theme headings, and 72,000 links to bible references. Hymns by 7,400 authors can be easily identified. The opening notes of 12,100 melodies are given and can be heard if users have a sound card, with those by 7,400 composers searchable. There are 119,000 entries showing the books in which the items are available in hard copy, 2,800 sets of biographical notes with 168 photographs. As well as 5,500 public domain texts, there are no less than 9,500 copyright texts, including the latest texts from many contemporary hymn-writers. All of Fred Pratt Green's texts, except for a few unsuitable for general use, are there.

These numbers clearly indicate the scale of the Trustees' vision. The extensive and sophisticated searching facilities enable users to pull out what they are looking for at a click of the mouse. This is primarily a tool for use in preparing worship in church, but is useful too, not only to students of hymnody, but all individuals interested in hymns. A reading programme is provided, supplying for 2001 choices of modern hymns, one selected for 365 of the 2,000 themes. This is just one of a series of articles, bible studies and related material in a *Hymnopaedia* section which comes as a bonus to the main database.

Bernard Braley: *HymnQuest*

HymnQuest is more than a tremendous resource for finding hymns and tunes for occasions of all kinds: its *Hymnopaedia* section contains, alongside other treasures, a series of Bible Studies round the words of eleven hymns. More will be added, and the study below is one due to appear in January 2002. Alan Luff has prepared this study based on one of Fred's hymns.

> An Upper Room did our Lord prepare
> for those he loved until the end:
> and his disciples still gather there
> to celebrate their Risen Friend.
>
> A lasting gift Jesus gave his own:
> to share his bread, his loving cup.
> Whatever burdens may bow us down,
> he by his Cross shall lift us up.
>
> And after Supper he washed their feet
> for service, too, is sacrament.
> In him our joy shall be made complete –
> sent out to serve, as he was sent.
>
> No end there is! We depart in peace,
> he loves beyond the uttermost:
> in every room in our Father's house
> he will be there as Lord and Host.

Principal Passages for reading

Mark 14, 12–25
Luke 22, 14–23
John 13, 1–17; 14, 1–4
I Corinthians 11, 23–26

The mention of an 'upper room' is confined to three places in the New Testament. The statement in *Mark*, which St Luke closely follows, indicates that the arrangements for the preparation for the sharing of the Passover meal were made in an Upper Room: the reference in *Acts* 1, 13 to an upper room that the apostles were using as a kind of headquarters in the days immediately after his Resurrection. Later in *Acts* we find Peter returning home to some such headquarters (*Acts* 12, 12) described as the home of Mary mother of Mark. In that case this may be the room where Jesus appeared to the disciples who had locked themselves in 'for fear of the Jews' (*Luke* 24, 33; *John* 20, 19), and where according to John the Holy Spirit was given to them. And was this the house that was shaken by 'the mighty rushing wind' at Pentecost?

Clearly the 'Upper Room' is an image full of meaning in the New Testament and in the minds of many Christians, as a place of retreat and sanctuary, a place of meeting with fellow Christians and with their Lord, above all the Risen Lord. But the Upper Room was a place of both retreat and challenge. FPG takes up the sense of sanctuary in the first verse of the hymn, adding the reference from *John* 13, 1 concerning the love of Jesus for his disciples.

In fact the prevailing atmosphere of the hymn throughout is that of the account in St John's Gospel of Jesus' last evening with his disciples. Verse 3 moves to the washing of the disiples' feet. Verse 4 has an unmistakable reference to *John* 14.

continued on next page

AN UPPER ROOM

But FPG picks up the reference in *John* 13, 4 that there was a supper and that it was during the supper that Jesus washed his disciples' feet. John has no account of the institution of the Eucharist. Clearly however he knows the Eucharist in the Church intimately. There is no fuller exposition of its meaning than that in *John* 6, where Jesus follows the Feeding of the Five Thousand with his teaching (6, 35) that he himself is 'the Bread of life', and in *John* 15 where he declares, 'I am the true Vine'. So verse 2 speaks of the Last Supper and the 'lasting gift' of the sacrament that Jesus gave his 'own', his disciples then, the faithful Church today. FPG moves in the last two lines to what may indeed be his own experience of receiving the sacrament, that it enables us to bear burdens. But his move of thought from the sacrament to the cross echoes the earliest account of the institution of the sacrament in *I Corinthians* 11, 23–26 where Paul declares that whenever we partake we 'proclaim the death of the Lord until he comes'.

But though the Upper Room may be a place of spiritual sanctuary it is also a place of challenge, and our experience at the Sacrament, though one of the most intimate and personal things in our lives is by no means to be an enclosed experience. In verse 3 we have the disciples having their feet washed by their Lord. But this too was not a matter to be hugged each to themselves as a purely personal privilege. Immediately he had set aside the towel and taken his place amongst them Jesus drew out the lesson that it is service to one another that will show their greatest likeness to him.

And so the final verse begins with a memorable declaration of the openness of the life of those who receive the body and blood of Christ, 'No end is here'. We are now momentarily with every local church, coming to end of their time of being apart to celebrate the Sacrament. We depart in peace, having received the outward sign of the utter love of God that can prevail even when inwardly we are full of doubt and hesitation.

There remains, necessarily for the understanding of the Eucharist, a final couplet. This sacrament is not for all eternity. It is for this time of separation, while we wait and long for the time when God will be all in all. On that last night in the Upper Room Jesus had a word on this too. The disciples expressed their anxiety when Jesus said that he would be leaving them; he responded by promising a place in his Father's house, that place with many dwelling places, where he himself will be present to preside for all eternity as the Host of his own feast.

As we leave our local place of meeting with our fellow Christians, separating from them, and going into a world where what we have just done may be very little understood, we need both of these final emphases from the hymn. We need to know that we go out to serve. We may quote another great hymn for the end of the Eucharist, close perhaps to FPG's heart, Charles Wesley's words:

> Forth in thy name. O Lord, I go,
> my daily labour to pursue,
> thee, only thee, resolved to know
> in all I think, or speak, or do.

But in all the struggles of daily life we need to know that at the End as at the Beginning, there is Jesus, who will welcome us as 'Lord and Host'.

Alan Luff

A LITANY OF THANKSGIVING

For God's servant, Frederick Pratt Green, preacher, pastor, poet, playwright, hymn-writer, wit and teacher.
Made, like all human beings, in the image of God.

Holy Bible: Old Testament

For God's gift of freewill to all human creatures and God's expectation that his creatures should accept responsibility for their actions.
For if, made like some android race, though warm with flesh and blood, our happy self, with smiling face was programmed to be good, and had no freedom, seeing wrong, to choose it, or say no, our praise would be a puppet-song, and love an empty show.

Brian Wren

For Fred's understanding and experience of Jesus, suffering servant, his death on the Cross and his Resurrection leading him to state that Love is another name for God.
Son of God, if thy free grace again has raised me up, keep me, keep me, gracious Lord, and never let me go.

Charles Wesley

For Fred's discovery that revelations of God's truth can be found in the holy books of all religions; and in the writings of prophets, philosophers and mystics, ancient and modern. For his understanding that such knowledge both confirms that all human beings are made in God's image and saves us all from uninformed bigotry about those who do not believe what we believe.
Gather us in, we worship only Thee, in varied names, we stretch a common hand, in diverse forms, a common soul we see, in many ships we seek one spirit-land, gather us in!

George Matheson

For Fred's humility in acknowledging the great gift of God's Holy Spirit informing and empowering his own creativity.
We did it between us, the good Lord and I.

Joseph Scriven

For Fred, the constant learner, never too young, never too old to welcome new insights from God and God's other creatures.
Let us wear L-plates all our days in lively anticipation of growth in wisdom and stature.

Bernard Braley

For Fred's understanding of the importance of partnerships, between lyricists and composers, between hymn-writers and congregations; between playwrights, actors and audiences, between poets and readers and between writers and publishers.
Poet, painter, music-maker, all your treasures bring, florist, actor, graceful dancer, make your offering: join your hands in celebration, let creation shout and sing!

David Mowbray

For Fred's belief that all true relationships are two-way, a giving and a receiving from one another.
Parents, offspring, friends and neighbours, born to give and to receive; charged by Christ to bear his image, full maturity achieve, in the discipline of matching intertwining gifts and needs, growing in their Master's likeness proving faith with lovers' deeds.

Bernard Braley

For Fred's example of revering the past, enjoying the present and welcoming the future.
Thou art love's unfathomed ocean, wisdom's deepest, clearest sea, heaven's and earth's salvation portion, Parent of eternity; grace and glory in abundance flow from Thee.

Lilian Watkins

For Fred's respect for the natural world, his love of flowers, animals and landscape, his concern about pollution and greed harming our God-given earth.
A beanfield full in blossom smells as sweet as Araby, or groves of orange flowers, black-eyed and white, and feathered to one's feet, how sweet they smell in morning's dewy hours! When seething night is left upon the flowers, and when morn's sun shines brightly o'er the field, the bean bloom glitters in the gems of showers, and sweet the fragrance which the union yields to battered footpaths crossing o'er the fields.

John Clare

For Fred's diverse gifts of humour, integrity, generosity, compassionate observation of detail, appreciation of non-orthodoxy and above all for his ordinariness.
For it was his extraordinary ordinariness that enabled all who met him face to face or through his writing to recognise a common humanity. Thanks be to God.

This libretto for a short cantata is based on The Letters to the Seven Churches in *Revelation* chapters 2 and 3. The order in which the seven churches occur in the Biblical text seems to have been dictated by the route the messenger would have to take. There is one change of order, placing Philadelphia last, instead of Laodicea. The text is simplified by leaving out some passages which are obscure or have no relevance for today. A commentary is added, sung antiphonally by the choir, to provide a necessary local background to what is the eternal message of the Spirit to the Church in all ages.

The script is for two voices (the second given in italic type). The choral material (given in bold type) may be spoken or sung.

It was on the Lord's Day that I, John, your
    brother,
a prisoner, for preaching Christ, on the Isle of
    Patmos,
during the persecution of Christians in the reign
    of Nero,
heard behind me a voice like the sound of a
    trumpet, saying:

*Write in a letter the things which the Spirit tells
    you,*
*and send it to these seven churches in the
    Province of Asia:*
Ephesus;
Smyrna;
Pergamum;
Thyatira;
Sardis;
Laodicea;
Philadelphia.

I: THE CHURCH THAT HAS LOST
ITS FIRST LOVE: EPHESUS

Great Ephesus! Diana's Shrine!
How commerce thrives on things divine:
a populous city, proud to be
vested with Rome's authority,
Asia's metropolis – and free.

The Church of Christ in such a place,
where every sect sets up its stall,
has need to pray for special grace.
We preach Christ crucified for all,
as taught by his great apostle Paul.

Hear, you who have ears to hear, what the
Spirit is saying to the Church at Ephesus:

I know your ways!
You have fortitude and have not flagged.
You have not been fooled by false prophets:
but I have this against you:
You have lost your first love.
Repent, and serve me as you did at the first!

II: THE CHURCH THAT IS AFRAID OF
PERSECUTION: SMYRNA

Not every city, like our own,
rises again when overthrown,
For this we have to thank the Jews,
who next to making money, choose
to spend their time denouncing Jews!

How hard to preach the Gospel here,
where friends are foes; and all conspire
to make us hostages to fear.
God save us if we have to walk through fire!

Hear, you who have ears to hear, what the
Spirit is saying to the Church at Smyrna:

I know all your ways!
how hard pressed you are – and poor:
yet you are rich.
Be not afraid of the suffering to come.
Only be faithful unto death
and I will give you the crown of life.

III: THE CHURCH THAT IS HOLDING
FAST: PERGAMUM

How proud we are of Pergamum!
for here Augustus first became
the god to whom all knees must bow.
Approach the altar, make your vow:
there is no greater god than Rome!

Alas, our brother Antipas is dead,
true servant of the Crucified.
May it be said of us: not one denied
that Jesus is Lord, though all have died.

Hear, you who have ears to hear, what the
Spirit is saying to the Church at Pergamum:

I know all your ways!
I know where you live: it is the place
where Satan has his throne.
And yet you are holding fast to my cause,
and did not deny your faith in me
when Antipas, my faithful witness,
was killed in your city.

IV: THE CHURCH THAT IS DOING BETTER
THAN AT FIRST: THYATIRA

**The Guilds of Thyatira claim
their workmanship is next to none.
All Asia knows they have a name
for devilry when work is done!**

**Pray for our workers as they meet
the pressures of a pagan world:
its temple lusts contaminate
the air we breathe, the food we eat.**

Hear, you who have ears to hear, what the
Spirit is saying to the Church at Thyatira:

*I know all your ways!
I know your love and faithfulness,
your good service and your fortitude;
and you are doing better than at first.
But I have this against you:
you tolerate the Jezebel who is tempting you to
    conform.
Hold fast what you have till I come!*

V: THE CHURCH THAT IS SPIRITUALLY DEAD:
SARDIS

**Look up at Sardis on its hill:
our fortress seems impregnable.
Yet twice our adversary crept
upon us as the watchmen slept,
to burn and ravage, rape and kill.**

**The Church, of course, seeks to obey
what Christ commands, yet everyday,
and everywhere, is sorely pressed.
But grant us this: we do our best!**

Hear, you that have ears to hear, what the
Spirit is saying to the Church at Sardis:

*I know all your ways!
You have a name for being alive:
but you are dead. Wake up!
Strengthen what is left before it dies:
for I have not found any work of yours
completed in the eyes of my God.*

VI: THE CHURCH THAT IS LUKEWARM:
LAODICEA

**We Ladoiceans have no need
to grovel for imperial aid.
Even the earthquake did not shake
our banks; and every claim is paid.**

**The Church, of course, shares this success.
Collections show a marked increase;
Our altar cross is purest gold.
Offending none, we meet in peace.**

Hear, you who have ears to hear, what the
Spirit is saying to the Church at Laodicea:

*I know all your ways!
You are neither hot nor cold.
Because you are lukewarm,
I will spit you out of my mouth.*

*You say: how rich I am!
How well I have done!
I have everything I want!*

*I advise you to buy of me true gold,
and white clothes to hide your shame,
and ointment to open your eyes.*

*Those I love I reprove and discipline.
Be on your mettle and repent!*

VII: THE CHURCH THAT HAS BEFORE IT
AN OPEN DOOR: PHILADELPHIA

**Our city, Philadelphia lies
where many roads converge and meet:
armies and traders come and go;
the whole world jostles in our street.**

**So few of us! so great the task!
We long to see the Good News spread
down every road where soldiers tramp,
down every road that traders tread.**

Hear, you who have ears to hear, what the
Spirit is saying to the Church at Philadelphia:

*I know all your ways!
Your strength is small,
but you have kept my commands and have not
    disowned my name.
Look! I have set before you an Open Door,
which no one can shut.
Hold fast what you have;
let no one rob you of your crown.*

These are the words of the Holy One, the true
    One.
When he opens, none may shut;
when he shuts, none may open.

**Hear, you who have ears to hear, what the
Spirit is saying to us.
Amen.**

(A Knocking)

Who knocks? Who knocks so late on my Inn door?
Full many we have, lad, and can take no more!

O Master, 'tis a Lady fair,
And her Man, Joseph, who knock there;
Nor any lodging can she buy
In Bethlehem, though her hour is nigh.

Take them, lad, to the stable bare,
Sir Joseph and this Lady fair,
To-night no other room have we
For Jesu, His Nativity.

(A Knocking)

Who knocks? Who knocks so loud on my Inn door?
Full many we have, lad, and can take no more!

O Master, in the wintry air
Stand simple shepherds knocking there,
Who quit their watching for to see
King Jesu, His Nativity.

No King have we, but a Baby small
Born this night in a manger stall;
Light the lamp, lad, they shall see
King Jesu, His Nativity!

(A Knocking)

Who knocks? Who knocks so loud on my Inn door?
Full many we have, lad, and can take no more!

O gentle Master, knocking there
Are three Wise Kings, with gifts so rare,
From very far they come, to see
King Jesu, His Nativity.

Then up, lad! Set your lamp alight
For 'tis a very darksome night,
That these three Kings may gaze upon
Mary, and Jesu Christ her Son.

(A Knocking)

Who knocks? Who knocks to-night on my Inn door?
Full many we have, lad, and can take no more!

O Master, in the frosty air
All the world is knocking there,
Come on this Christmas night to see
King Jesu, His Nativity.

Then light the lamp, lad! All shall share
The worship of this King so fair.
Come all you people, kneel and see
Jesu our King's Nativity!

Fred Pratt Green: *A Carol*
Written for Christmas celebrations at Hunmanby Hall
School during Fred's chaplaincy (1928–1931).

Where the tides of humanity ebb and flow
In streets within sound of the sea,
Said the Lord to his faithful in Brighton Town:
'These people are precious to me!'

So, a century since, for the love of Christ,
They built us a church within reach
Of the shepherdless multitudes passing by,
And gave us a gospel to preach.

The records are there, if we care to read;
And faces that move us to say:
'No wonder God honoured their simple faith,
And prospered the work in their day.'

For those who are ready to do his will
What challenges God has in store:
In a Regency stable to offer Christ!
But how many came in by that door.

Then let us rejoice in what God has done:
Encouraged, yet never content;
Let us plan for tomorrow a fresh advance,
And pray for the Spirit's descent.

Fred Pratt Green: *A Hymn for the Centenary of*
Dorset Gardens Methodist Church in June 1985.
Tune: DORSET GARDENS especially written by the
organist Malcolm Davey.

* * * * *

Brothers and Sisters, it is right to raise
Our voices in enjoyment of past days;
To greet our Founders, each and all of them
Who strove to build God's New Jerusalem.

What they believed in, lest we should forget,
We meet to celebrate, as they once met:
In fellowship to spur each other on
Until what God has purposed shall be done.

Brothers and Sisters, movements come and go;
They sweep us forward, lose momentum, slow;
Their clarion calls the wind has blown away:
New perils threaten a more dangerous day.

Led by the Spirit, source of all good deeds,
We turn from old concerns to present needs:
May God who blessed our Founders grant us grace
To find in our new world a useful place.

Fred Pratt Green: *For the Wisbech Brotherhood's*
80th birthday.
Written May 1987. Tune: SURSUM CORDA

The Sons of Asaph, Scripture says,
Were in their place that day of days
When one good king at last restored
The worship of the one true God:
Sing Alleluia!

Who Asaph was, you rightly guess:
A Chief Musician, nothing less,
Who taught his choir a God to please,
With cymbals, harps and psalteries:
Sing Alleluia!

And future choirs that bore his name,
Like him, made excellence their aim;
A hundred strong, they took their place,
And sang the songs of sovereign grace:
Sing Alleluia!

So God be thanked, these sullen days,
For all who still inspire our praise,
Who teach the arts that God has given
To lift our souls from earth to heaven:
Sing Alleluia!

Then let us cherish, more and more,
Our right to worship and adore,
In hymnody and psalms and songs
The God to whom all life belongs:
Sing Alleluia!

Fred Pratt Green: *The Sons of Asaph*. 2 Chronicles
35, 15.
When Fred was asked in 1989 to write a hymn
celebrating the twenty years of Russell and
Suzanne Schulz-Widmar's service to their
United Methodist Church in Austin, Texas, he
remembered a sermon he used to preach at choir
anniversaries on 'The Sons of Asaph' and how he
once tried to write a hymn of thankfulness for the
musicians who have enriched the worship of the
Church through the centuries. What better occasion
than this to have another go!
It gave Fred great pleasure that Jane Marshall was
invited to write the tune ASAPH for this text.

* * * * *

Love it is unites us
On our wedding day,
Love it is rejoices
In the vows we say;
Christ it is who blesses
Bridegroom and bride,
As they kneel before him,
Side by side.

We must trust each other;
Worthy be of trust:
Learn to share life's riches,
And its crust.
Christ at his own Table
Knows how to provide,
As we kneel before him,
Side by side.

If the path we follow
Suddenly grows steep,
If in winter weather
Snow lies deep:
Christ behind to guard us,
Christ before to guide,
We shall make the journey,
Side by side.

Fred Pratt Green: *Side by Side*
Written 5th November 1989 for the tune
CRANHAM.

* * * * *

Simple shepherds, what brings you here
This night to Bethlehem?
To see a Babe at Mary's breast,
As thirsty as any lamb.

Joyful shepherds, your happiness
Is catching as the fever!
We share the joy that Mary has
Now lambing time is over.

Kneeling shepherds, do you not see
The Babe is fast asleep?
One day the Lamb of God will be
Our Shepherd, we his sheep.

Troubled shepherds, why must you leave
The shelter of the manger?
The wolves are howling on the hill,
And lambs may be in danger.

Fred Pratt Green: *A Carol for the Lamb of God*
On an undated Christmas card to his wife.
Inscribed 'Young Love may be exciting but there is
nothing to equal Old Love! Love from, Ever your
own, Derry' (followed by seven kisses).

* * * * *

How many servants of the Lord,
In secret discontent,
Await his clear, decisive word –
Then go where they are sent.

Some welcome change, or suffer it,
Fearful of losing friends;
All ask themselves if they are fit
To meet life's new demands.

May Christ, in whom we work and rest,
Grant to his servant Ann,
In her new life, a life more blest
Than she has power to plan.

To God the Father, God the Son,
And God the Spirit, praise!
May acts of love, cheerfully done
Fill all our faithful days!

Fred Pratt Green: *For Ann Cubitt*
Written July 1990. Tune: DUNDEE

Give God the glory, Christ the praise,
For saints in these, and former days,
Who in a time of stress and strife
Trust by their reconciling life,
When creeds divide, to heal and bind,
And reach, in Christ, a common mind.

Two Christian missions sought to win
A pagan Mercia from its sin:
One counting Lindisfarne its home,
The other sent from distant Rome,
One beauty-loving and more free,
One grounded in authority.

A boy at Lindisfarne, when grown
Became the saint we call our own:
A man of gentleness and peace,
He grieved that discord should increase:
At Whitby wanted to preserve
That one true Church he lived to serve.

A man the King had come to trust,
He loved his flock, as shepherds must;
When slighted, turned the other cheek
(How blest, said Jesus, are the meek):
Who at his death was Bishop here,
Whose name we honour and revere.

Lord, in this shrine may we proclaim
The faith that justifies the fame
Of Chad, who would rejoice to see
True growth in Christian unity,
And prompt us by our lives to prove
Christ's is an all-embracing love.

Fred Pratt Green: *A Hymn in Honour of Saint Chad*
Written 1990 for a celebration in Lichfield Cathedral

* * * * *

Lord Jesus, take this child,
So briefly in our care,
Into your eternal world
To breathe its purer air.

And, as you shared their grief
Who mourned for Lazarus,
In our own time of sudden loss,
Comfort and strengthen us.

Bless those who seek to heal
All kinds of human pain;
And all who do not lose their faith,
Though mysteries remain.

As praying turns to praise,
Together we adore
The God who wipes away our tears
And bids us grieve no more.

Fred Pratt Green: *A Hymn for Thomas and his Parents*
Written in 1990 for the funeral of baby Thomas,
who died in infancy after an earlier infant death of
baby Daniel. Recommended Tune: FRANCONIA

He was homeless in our world,
Born for us of Mary's womb:
Jesus! Jesus!
Help us make your kingdom come.

They are his, the homeless ones,
Victims of our tribal strife:
Children! Children!
Is this all you know of life?

They are his, the starving ones
Suckled at a milkless breast:
Children ! Children!
While you suffer, who can rest?

They are his, the orphaned ones,
Prisoners of uncaring care:
Children! Children!
Rouse us by your mute despair.

He was helpless in our world,
Born for us of Mary's womb:
Jesus! Jesus!
Help us make your kingdom come.

Fred Pratt Green: *Save the Children*
Written 1990 for the tune FINGEST by John
Barnard described by Fred as very beautiful.

* * * * *

How ancient our church, still here on its hill,
Ten centuries old and witnessing still,
Where Christians together go down on their knees
To find, in repentance, forgiveness and peace.

From Doomsday till now it has served as a fold
To shelter Christ's flock in troubles untold,
Of invasion, oppression, injustice and greed,
In times of contention in worship and creed.

For Christ never lacks, today as of yore,
Those servants of his who care for the poor,
Whose lives of compassion still answer our doubt
By showing us clearly what life is about.

So let us revere John the Baptist, our saint,
Who startled the crowds with his call to repent,
Foreseeing in Jesus one greater than he,
The nation's Messiah, our saviour to be.

Then let us proclaim the eternal Good News,
That promise of God we accept or refuse,
And prove by our actions, all saints on our side,
We trust in salvation, through Christ crucified.

Fred Pratt Green: *A Hymn for Old Lakenham Parish Church*
Written 1990. Tune: PADERBORN

God's servants of old,
Religious and lay,
Because they believed
To work is to pray,
In church and cathedral
Knew how to create
Perspectives of beauty
That cry 'God is great!'

What treasures the past
Has laid at our feet!
What truths to defend,
What tasks to complete!
Our task is restoring,
With patience and joy,
Things time and pollution
Deface and destroy.

Now many there are
Who share this concern,
Who proffer their skills,
Or offer to learn.
When working is worship
It matters no more
That some climb a ladder,
And some scrub a floor!

Lord, grant us the grace,
In practical ways,
To capture afresh
The spirit of praise,
And find in a growing
Respect for the past,
In Christian commitment
A faith that shall last.

Fred Pratt Green: *A Hymn for the Anniversary
Celebration of Cathedral Camps on 15 May 1991*
Tune: OLD 104TH

Fred indicates that an earlier and not so serious
version of this text was submitted to and accepted
by the Cathedral Campers but that it did not prove
acceptable to the authorities at Saint Paul's
Cathedral, London, where the service took place.
The words, given below, were to be sung to
SUSSEX CAROL.

Our great cathedrals, built in days
Of simple faith, were acts of praise:
Now time and our polluted air
Are putting them beyond repair.
Will someone help? How did you guess?
Cathedral Campers answered 'Yes!'

Now holidays are holy days,
And jobs are nearly acts of praise,
As Campers, climbing ladders, wear
The season's styles in safety gear,
While lesser mortals seek to please
By scrubbing floors upon their knees.

And Campers, working without pay,
While drawing breath are heard to say:
'What gets me beat is how those monks
Man-handled such enormous chunks
Of wood and stone and placed them there.
It must have been the power of prayer!'

So understanding slowly grows
Why monks, without computers, chose
To spend their lives in acts of praise
And learning skills by which to raise
These wonders of a bygone age,
Now our endangered heritage.

* * * * *

'One of the children of the year'
Is the little Lord Jesus:
One of us, yet a stranger here,
Is the little Lord Jesus:
One of us, but of special birth,
Is the little Lord Jesus.
God's only Son shall walk the earth!

'One of the children of the year'
Is the little Lord Jesus:
Mary and Joseph are taking care
Of the little Lord Jesus:
One of us, yet the Saviour of all,
Is the little Lord Jesus.
Watch his first footsteps, lest he fall!

'One of the children of the year'
Is the little Lord Jesus:
Look, the day-star is shining clear
For the little Lord Jesus:
Look at that shadow of a cross –
O my little Lord Jesus!
Look, he holds out his hands to us!

Fred Pratt Green: *One of the Children of the Year*
The first line is a quotation from a poem by Alice
Meynell. Written in July 1991 for a competition in
The Methodist Recorder inviting tunes. The winner
was Ronald Watson and the carol is available from
Stainer & Bell.

* * * * *

Welcome to this world of ours,
To the world you gave us.
Alleluia,
Jesus comes to save us!
Though the best that we can offer
Is a dusty manger:
Joy and peace!
Joseph shall keep you from all danger.

Welcome to this life of ours,
To the life you gave us.
Alleluia,
Jesus comes to save us!
All the food that we can offer
Is our homely best:
Joy and peace!
Mary shall feed you at her breast.

Welcome to these hearts of ours,
To the self you gave us.
Alleluia,
Jesus comes to save us!
Though the love that I can offer
Is but weak and poor:
Joy and peace!
Jesus is knocking at my door.

Fred Pratt Green: *The Welcome Carol*
Written for the choir of Burton-on-Trent Methodist
Church, July 1991. A musical setting of these words
was also written later by Valerie Ruddle.

* * * * *

One hundred years! a time to pause
before we celebrate the cause
we have so much at heart.
How little could have been achieved,
had we, and others, not believed
each plays a useful part.

Then let us thank the living Lord
for all who seek to spread the Word,
and make the meaning plain;
for every art that reaches out
to those who fall and those who doubt,
and lifts them up again.

When poet and musician share
a clear intention to declare
what God has freely given,
and choir and congregation raise
their voices in whole-hearted praise:
how close we are to heaven!

How close to heaven, and yet alive
to pray, to plan, and daily strive
to serve the God we praise,
by using new, and ancient, skills,
as those believing God fulfils
himself in many ways.

One hundred or a thousand years,
whoever speaks, or sings, or hears,
the Gospel is the same:
that one alone has power to save,
who gives the faith we need to have,
and Jesus is his name.

Fred Pratt Green: *For a Centenary Celebration*
Written 1992. Suggested tune: HULL

* * * * *

The wind of the Spirit
Still blows where it will;
Without inspiration
What use is our skill?
Joe Scriven, Joe Scriven,
How humbly you cry:
'We did it between us
The good Lord and I!'

You suffered the worst
Human love can endure,
Not once but twice lost
A love that was sure:
Yet out of bereavement,
Your faith holding fast,
You wrote for our comfort
A song that shall last.

Verse 1 of 'What a friend we have in Jesus' is sung

The wind of the Spirit
Still blows where it will,
And never an artist
But prays for it still;
And never an author
But waits for a spark
Of pure inspiration
To banish the dark.

The mystery grows!
It's hard to assess
In realms of the Spirit
The greater or less.
Joe Scriven, Joe Scriven,
Who dares to deny:
'We did it between us
The good Lord and I!'

Fred Pratt Green: *The Spirit and Joseph Scriven*
Written June 1992. Tune: PADERBORN

* * * * *

How great a debt we owe
We Christians of today,
To those who understood
It's not enough to pray,
Who planned and worked and sacrificed
To share with us their faith in Christ.

So when the nightmare years
Were over, barriers down,
And populations spread
Beyond our Brighton Town,
In Woodingdean a faithful few
Began a work that quietly grew.

Now in a time of change
For good as well as ill,
When subtle dangers test
Even the strongest will:
How clear our witness has to be,
How vital Christian unity!

Therefore we pledge ourselves
To make the Gospel known
Between the Downs and sea,
To reap what has been sown,
And be a Church prepared to face
Another thousand years of grace.

Fred Pratt Green: *A Hymn for Woodingdean*
Written October 1992

Where but in God does caring start,
That urgency of mind and heart
To meet a human need?
And did not Jesus stress above
All else the practice of such love
In what he said and did?

Rejoice that in a world at war
Those whom we honour now foresaw
What they must make their aim:
To end the loneliness and fears
Of those who in their later years
Need refuge and a home.

Once caring starts, how caring grows!
We cannot turn aside from those
Life handicaps and maims:
And science offers us new skills
To combat old and modern ills,
And multiplies our aims.

Then let us share the work in hand
With all who care and understand
What is our present task,
Believing God will surely bless
Work done in loving faithfulness,
And give the strength we ask.

Fred Pratt Green: *A Hymn to Celebrate Fifty Years of Caring by Methodist Homes for the Aged*
Written for a celebration in Wesley's Chapel on 14 March 1993. Tune: HULL

* * * * *

This vision of peace
how old and how new!
The greater our need,
the clearer it grew.
Yet side-by-side nations,
drummed-up to resist,
still glare across frontiers
that cease to exist.

This vision of peace
is making us one;
no longer we ask
who lost and who won.
Concern for each other
is healing old wounds,
for all is forgiven
when goodwill abounds.

This vision of peace
is ours from above;
it springs from the heart
of a crucified love.
Deride it, defeat it,
it shames our despairs,
how blest are peacemakers,
God's Kingdom is theirs!

Fred Pratt Green: *A Vision of Peace*
Written for publication in the Methodist magazine *Magnet*, July 1993. Tune: PADERBORN

How many friends there are in Christ
Who never see each other's face,
Who never meet in daily life,
Or share in worship in one place.

Strangers they are, in very truth
And strangers they may always be,
Yet neighbours could not be more close
Than those who share Christ's unity.

For was not this our Lord's concern,
That all his followers should be one?
How well he knew that all he did
In his own name could be undone.

Then let us greet our unseen friends,
Who meet in worship near and far,
And prove, with them, though so unlike,
How truly one we Christians are.

Fred Pratt Green: *A Hymn for Mellish Road Methodist Church, Walsall*
Written September 1993

* * * * *

When Jesus' ministry began
In field and market place,
With news of God's redeeming plan
For all the human race,
He came from years at bench and lathe,
He'd lived by what he earned,
And clothed the words of heavenly faith
In wisdom he had learned.

To help his hearers understand
God's kingdom and the Way,
He spoke of farmers and their land,
Of children and their play.
From fish and flowers, from weeds and wine,
And wandering sheep, He drew
A picture of a love divine
From things his people knew.

He chose to trust his kingdom's keys
To Simon Peter's hands.
Through fishermen and folk like these
His gospel reached all lands.
And through the Church's history,
Upheld in faithfulness
The Lord has used lay ministry
To save and heal and bless.

A God who rules the firmament,
Yet lived and worked on earth,
Makes all our life a sacrament
Anoints our work with worth.
You are a God of majesty
A God all gods above,
But it is your humanity
That lifts our hearts in love.

Fred Pratt Green: Written for a competition for hymns to celebrate 200 years of recognition of Methodist Local Preachers, 1996. Tune: SAINT WULFSTAN

GENERAL INDEX
All works by Fred Pratt Green unless otherwise shown

ACKNOWLEDGEMENTS & COPYRIGHT

The publishers are grateful to those who have given permission for copyright material to be included. Every effort has been made to trace copyright owners, and apologies are extended to anyone whose rights have inadvertently not been acknowledged.

The hymns, carols and poems by Fred Pratt Green which are printed in full in this volume and are indicated by a * in the General Index are controlled by Stainer & Bell Ltd, 23 Gruneisen Road, London N3 1DZ for the world except USA and Canada and by Hope Publishing Company, 380 South Main Place, Carol Stream, Illinois 60188, USA for the USA and Canada. All extracts from hymns printed on pages 62, 77, 78 & 79 are similarly controlled.

The hymns, carols and poems and other writing by Fred Pratt Green indicated by a † in the General Index are controlled by Stainer & Bell Ltd for the world.

The following material is included by permission as shown below and is listed in order of appearance in the book:

page vi:	Photograph by permission of Jacqueline Wyatt, Norwich.
page 3:	Child (Sydney Carter). By permission of Stainer & Bell Ltd.
page 10:	Extracts from *The Rydalian* and photograph of A. G. Watt. By permission of the Governers of Rydal Penrhos School.
page 30:	Photograph by permission of Owen Waters.
page 32:	Drawing of Pool-in-Wharfedale Methodist Church by permission of the artist, Jean Beever.
page 35:	Drama (Maureen Harris). By permission of the author.
page 41:	Personae (Fallon Webb). Copyright owner not traced.
page 42:	November in Hollywood (Elizabeth Shepherd). By permission of the author.
page 42:	Darling Two (Elizabeth Shepherd). By permission of the author.
page 45:	Death of a Scarecrow (Peter Dunn). By permission of Ruby Dunn.
page 46:	Holiday (Sydney Tremayne).Copyright owner not traced.
page 48:	Craig y Aderyn (Mark Bourne). By permission of the author.
page 50:	Drawing of Dorset Gardens Methodist Church by permission of the artist, Shirley Veater.
page 64:	Beneath the glory of the skies (Albert Bayly). © 1988 Oxford University Press. Used by permission.
page 64:	For the healing of the nations (Fred Kaan). By permission Hope Publishing Company (for USA and Canada) and Stainer & Bell Ltd for the rest of the world.
page 65:	Come, cradle all the future generations (Brian Wren). By permission of Hope Publishing Company (for USA, Canada, Australia and New Zealand) and Stainer & Bell Ltd for the rest of the world.
page 70:	Photograph by permission of Owen Waters.
page 81:	Music: Venture Gwen (Arranged by Mansel Thomas). By permission of Mansel Thomas Trust. Music available from Terence Gilmore-Jones, Ty Cerbyd, Station Road, Ponthir, Newport NP18 1GQ.
page 82:	Music: A Concert-goers' Carol. By permission of Stainer & Bell Ltd.
pages 91–3:	The Pratt Green Hymnology Collection at the University of Durham (Richard Watson). By permission of the author.
pages 94–5:	*HymnQuest* Bible Study (Alan Luff). By permission of the author.
page 96:	Extract from Revised English Bible. © Oxford University Press and Cambridge University Press 1989. Used by permission.
page 96:	Extract from Brian Wren hymn. By permission of Hope Publishing Company (USA, Canada, Australia and New Zealand) and Stainer & Bell for the rest of the world.
page 96:	Extracts from hymns by David Mowbray and Bernard Braley. By permission of Stainer & Bell Ltd.
page 99:	Where the tides of humanity ebb and flow. By permission of the Trustees of Dorset Gardens Methodist Church, Brighton.
page 99:	Brothers and Sisters, it is right to raise. By permission of the Wisbech Brotherhood, Wisbech Methodist Church, Wisbech.
page 101:	Give God the glory, Christ the praise. By permission of the Dean and Chapter of Lichfield Cathedral.
page 101:	How ancient our church, still here on its hill. By permission of Old Lakenham Parish Church, Norwich.
page 102:	God's servants of old. By permission of "Cathedral Camps".
page 103:	How great a debt we owe. By permission of the Trustees of Woodingdean Methodist Church, Brighton.
page 104:	Where but in God does caring start. By permission of Methodist Homes for the Aged.
page 104:	How many friends there are in Christ. By permission of the Trustees of Mellish Road Methodist Church, Walsall.

APPRECIATION

I acknowledge the considerable help of all those who have contributed to this book or led me to information about Fred's life and work. I received more remembrances than could be used, all showing the high esteem in which Fred Pratt Green was held. Appreciation is also expressed to those who have taken or supplied photographs for the book, or, over the years sent pictures that I have found in Fred's albums and papers. My thanks also go to Joyce Horn, who typed most of the original manuscript, and to the staff of Stainer & Bell, especially to Keith Wakefield, who designed the book, Carol Wakefield who oversaw the whole project and ensured extremely tight deadlines were met, Nicholas Williams, who made valuable suggestions, and Mandy Clifton who formatted the text in its final version. I am also grateful to the Trustees of The Pratt Green Trust who commissioned this book and to Alan Luff, who read my first draft, both for his encouragement and suggestions. It has been a joy and privilege to pay this inadequate tribute on behalf of all who travelled alongside Fred in his 97 years of mortal life.

Bernard Braley
London, March 2001